Critical acclaim for

THE ONE MINUTE WINE MASTER

by Jennifer Simonetti-Bryan, MW

"Who doesn't love quizzes? . . . Down to earth descriptions of wines and stress-free strategies for choosing them are among the topics covered. . . . It sure is fun!"   —*Good Housekeeping*

"Think of it as a Meyers-Briggs character assessment for wine nerds. . . . Simonetti-Bryan's personality quiz can help us understand our wine preferences and overcome reluctance to try something new."   —*Washington Post*

"A terrific introductory book for someone overwhelmed by wine options. . . . It's a Match.com for your palate, if you will."   —*Washington Examiner*

"Definitely educational . . . Simonetti-Bryan is trying to make wine tasting more accessible to people who may be overwhelmed by it. . . . It's a good primer for helping you grow into wine, and it's short enough to easily read through the first part and then focus on the wines recommended."   —The Good Wine Guru

"Easily approachable and non-threatening . . . The importance of understanding what kind of profile best fits you, owning that profile, and then celebrating it is an important addition to wine literature. . . . Enlightening . . . a great gift idea for the wine drinker . . . a thoughtful treat!"   —The Wine Cask

"Excellent for the wine newbie who wants to know what kind of wine he or she will probably like best."   —Wine Peeps

"A book to give to any beginner interested in learning about wine. It's a cross between a *Cosmopolitan* quiz and a *for Dummies*-style book. . . . A perfect gift."   —1,000 Corks

"A quick wine fix."   —*Publishers Weekly*

ROSÉ WINE

THE GUIDE TO DRINKING PINK

JENNIFER SIMONETTI-BRYAN, MW

STERLING EPICURE
New York

STERLING EPICURE
New York

An Imprint of Sterling Publishing Co., Inc.
1166 Avenue of the Americas
New York, NY 10036

ISBN 978-1-4549-2579-8

Distributed in Canada by Sterling Publishing Co., Inc.
c/o Canadian Manda Group, 664 Annette Street
Toronto, Ontario, M6S 2C8, Canada
Distributed in the United Kingdom by GMC Distribution Services
Castle Place, 166 High Street, Lewes, East Sussex, BN7 1XU, United Kingdom
Distributed in Australia by NewSouth Books
45 Beach Street, Coogee, NSW 2034, Australia

For information about custom editions, special sales, and premium and corporate purchases,
please contact Sterling Special Sales at 800-805-5489 or specialsales@sterlingpublishing.com.

Manufactured in Canada

2 4 6 8 10 9 7 5 3 1

www.sterlingpublishing.com

Interior design by Christine Heun

A complete list of image credits appears on page 170.

To my mother, Michele,
who always has rose-colored glasses
and asks, "Why not?"

CONTENTS

THE ROSÉ
⟩REVOLUTION⟨

Ask people to define rosé wine, and the answers will vary as widely as a field of wildflowers. They are still, fizzy, or sparkling. Their colors range from breathlessly pink to pale red. They run the gamut from almost weightless to full-bodied, low alcohol to high, velvety soft to sharply tart, and bone-dry to dessert sweet. Despite these vast variations in style, there's no denying the recent global explosion in the popularity of making and drinking pink wine.

Until recently, however, the world turned its collective nose up at rosé. Even within the last decade and in France, the wine capital of the world, rosé wines didn't receive much respect. "Rosés are not wine," said the sommelier of a Michelin-starred restaurant, with a tone of disgust, to Benjamin Lewin, a molecular biologist, master of wine, and author of *Wines of France* and *Wine Myths and Reality*.

But the world is changing. In 2014, per the International Organisation of Vine and Wine, global production of rosé accounted for nearly 10 percent of the industry, excluding sparkling wines. Four countries represent 80 percent of production, in descending order: France, Spain, America, and Italy. World consumption reached nearly 600 million gallons in 2014, a 20 percent increase since 2002. As of 2014, France and America drink the most, more than 200 million and 80 million gallons respectively.

Provence in particular, long renowned for its rosés, has seen tremendous growth in the last five years. *Fortune* magazine notes that exports from Provence have skyrocketed, soaring 58 percent in 2015 alone (see Figure 1). If you think that's a lot, consider that in 2001 the USA imported more than 40,000 gallons of rosé (see Figure 2). By 2015, that number had surpassed the 2 million–gallon mark, an almost incredulous increase of 4,852 percent! The value of imported rosés is increasing as well. Wineries worldwide are discovering how to reap serious profits from this crowd-pleasing drink.

In America, we view rosé largely as a seasonal wine. It generally hits shelves in late May or early June and leaves them by mid-September, but that's also changing. Now you can find and buy delicious rosés year-round.

So how did we get here?

FIGURE 1: PROVENCE ROSÉ EXPORTS TO AMERICA

■ MILLIONS OF LITERS OF WINE

Source: French customs agency and CIVP

FIGURE 2: SALES OF ROSÉ IMPORTED TO AMERICA

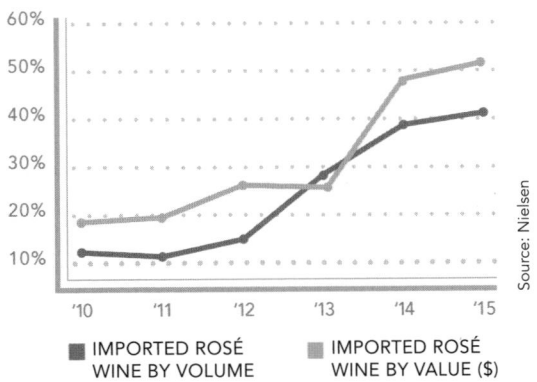

■ IMPORTED ROSÉ
WINE BY VOLUME

■ IMPORTED ROSÉ
WINE BY VALUE ($)

Source: Nielsen

A SHORT HISTORY OF ROSÉ

It doesn't help that the category has no universally agreed color, method, or style. Very pale Burgundies might qualify more as rosés, but we think of them as reds. Some aged white wines, such as Pinot Gris or Gewürztraminer, can take on a pink-orange hue, but, because they come from white grapes, technically they qualify as white wines.

Even just eight years ago, when I was studying for my master of wine (MW) qualification, finding information about rosé in books proved difficult. But the word "claret" kept popping up in various forms: *clairet, clarete, chiaretto*. Claret is the old English word for red Bordeaux wines, but it had a different connotation before that usage became prevalent. In the twelfth century, after the marriage of King Henry II of England to Eleanor of Aquitaine, France started exporting wine from Bordeaux to England. Then, the main style in Bordeaux was called *clairet*. The word derives from the Latin word *clarus*, meaning "clear," which means that for centuries red Bordeaux wines looked more like rosé than like the deep, rich red wines we see today.

Starting in the fourteenth century, the nobility and military leaders acquired and took control of many vineyards in Provence, which laid the foundations for the region's modern-day viticulture. The claret style soon grew in prestige, becoming the wine of kings and aristocrats. The rise of the railroad in the mid-nineteenth century created new accessibility and opened new markets for Provençal wine. At roughly the same time, however, the infamous phylloxera epidemic reached the region and devastated vineyards there. The plague traveled from north to south, wiping out virtually all native varieties that the pest encountered. Production plummeted as nearly all the vineyards of Europe succumbed to the infestation and diseases associated with it. Only vines growing in terrain composed principally of schist or sand escaped the devastation. Growers had to replant and start again.

St. Leobinus, patron saint of wine merchants, pours wine from a barrel into a serving vessel (stained glass window, Chartres Cathedral, late twelfth century).

Provence has a Mediterranean climate: mild winters, warm summers, lots of sunshine (3,000 hours a year!), and rain mainly in the fall and spring. As tourism flourished along the Côte d'Azur in the twentieth century, rosé production also increased. The 1956 movie *And God Created Woman* showcased Brigitte Bardot as a sensual eighteen-year-old nymphet lying around nude in her yard in St. Tropez, which further popularized the region. As the Cannes Film Festival grew in stature, it drew wine-loving celebrities here. The sexual revolution of the 1960s created a stir on Provençal beaches with the controversial monokini bathing suit, which attracted attention to the clothing-optional beaches. In America, however, people were still drinking whiskey.

Then, in the 1970s, Mateus, a lightly sweet rosé wine from Portugal, rose to fame and dominated the rosé scene in America with almost 4 million cases sold. It suited the collective American sweet tooth, and it had cachet. A famous photo (page 8) shows Jimi Hendrix chugging from the iconic Mateus bottle. Around the same time, the story goes that Queen Elizabeth, dissatisfied with the wine

Actress Jeanne Moreau stands on a table during the 1958 Cannes Film Festival.

selection at the Savoy Hotel, requested Mateus and the hotel manager had to send out for a bottle. When Hendrix and the queen are drinking the same stuff, you've got a hit. It was impossible for the world to dismiss drinking pink any longer.

While Mateus was reigning supreme, a new rosé—another blush—was preparing to conquer the scene. Some researchers believe that White Zinfandel resulted from a fermentation accident. Others suggest it gave winemakers a way to press profit from a by-product of intensifying their red Zinfandels. Either way, "White Zin" had an irreversible impact on the wine industry. Just one brand went from selling 25,000 cases in 1980 to more than 1.5 million by 1986.

Like most American kids, I grew up on Coca-Cola and Kool-Aid, so my first sip of dry red wine tasted sour and bitter. In the 1990s, my boyfriend's family hosted a Super Bowl party, and his mother was drinking wine, which seemed more sophisticated than soda or beer, simpler than cocktails, and less intense than pure spirits. The bottle from which she was drinking was labeled "White Zinfandel," and the wine tasted yummy. As with many Americans, "White Zin" opened the door for me to what seemed like a sophisticated, exclusive world.

Fast-forward to the new millennium, and you'll find another contender: Pink Moscato, also sweet, appealed to Gen Xers due in no small part to the hip-hop industry. Lil' Kim first rapped about it in her 2005 song "Lighters Up," but Drake receives most of the credit for putting Moscato on the map in 2009 with "Do It Now." After that, hip-hop artists name-dropped it seemingly everywhere, most recently in the chorus of a Waka Flocka Flame song and another featuring Kendrick Lamar. Pink Moscato caught fire. In 2014, Moscato

Jimi Hendrix swigs from a bottle of Mateus with girlfriend Kathy Etchingham.

accounted for 6.1 percent of the wine sold in U.S. food stores, and it has become one of the fastest-selling varietals in America. In California, Muscat Blanc acreage more than doubled from 2006 to 2013, and of all California table wine sold in America, Moscato increased 42 percent from 2011 to 2014.

While demand for Pink Moscato was running rampant, another celebrity pair affected the rosé world but on the dry side this time. Brad Pitt and Angelina Jolie purchased Château Miraval in Provence for $60 million in 2008. The wine that Miraval makes isn't just a pretty pink, though; it's good quality as well. *Wine Spectator* voted it the world's best rosé in 2012. The first run of 6,000 cases sold out within five hours of release, adding more dry fuel to the fire.

That same year, however, disaster struck. A news piece reported that the Hamptons—the collection of affluent towns in the east end of Long Island—ran out of dry rosé. The horror! Newspapers and TV networks nationwide ran tongue-in-cheek headlines about this unthinkable calamity. It happened again in 2014 and 2015; Page Six of *The New York Post*, *Vanity Fair*, *Good Morning America*—everyone was talking about it, and wine sellers and drinkers alike began looking beyond Provence for quality dry rosé.

THE FUTURE OF ROSÉ

This renewed demand has brought attention to the crowd-pleasing nature of rosé wines. More sommeliers are considering the category and including dry styles by the glass on their lists. Wine shops are keeping it on shelves not just during summer months but yearlong. The Hamptons Effect is paying dividends. New York now leads the nation in rosé consumption, representing 20 percent.

Château Miraval.

Because rosé is pink and wine, many people used to think of it as a drink for women, but it's making its way from bachelorette parties to tailgate parties. That's right, men are drinking pink: 2014 saw a 39 percent increase by volume in men drinking rosé. In fact, men now account for 45 percent of all U.S. rosé consumption, and, as more lifestyle journalists declare it cool, that number is growing.

In 2014, entertainment impresario Adam Carolla released a line of wine beverages called Mangria. It started as a traditional sangria plus vodka. "Then I started mixing batches and bringing it to Jimmy Kimmel's for Football Sunday, and people liked it," Carolla said to Teddy Durgin of *Beverage Journal*. It may have started as a joke, but it has blossomed into a legitimate business. They even make a pink Mangria called—wait for it—Brosé.

The Brosé Effect and the rise of frosé cocktails—which incorporate rosé and blended ice among other ingredients—are shaking up the wine industry, which for decades has marketed rosé primarily to women. Thankfully men and women alike are realizing that everyone can enjoy this delicious, varied, food-friendly wine. The future is looking bright and . . . pink!

GETTING STARTED

1

MAKING
⇒ ROSÉ ⇐

Rosé wines come in many shades, from barely pink to deep crimson. Most may look pink, but that doesn't mean they're all made the same way. Growing region, grape type, and production method all have an enormous influence on style and flavor. Let's take a closer look.

TERROIR

Terroir is the French word for how the locality or immediate area where a crop grows influences how it tastes. Altitude, soil, climate, and surrounding plant life all can affect terroir in measurable ways.

A blind tasting is when you taste one or more wines poured from identity-obscured bottles. (When I was studying for my MW, my husband poured them for me while I went into the next room so I couldn't cheat by seeing the color or shape of the bottle.) If I'm tasting blind, I try framing my first impression by the temperature of the growing climate. Warm climate wines have flavors of ripe, juicy, jammy, or even cooked fruit. Cool climate wines exhibit lighter, more acidic fruit flavors, such as lemon, lime, and grapefruit.

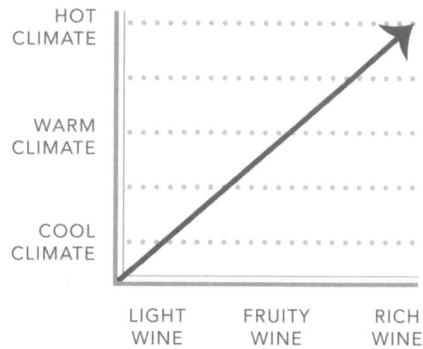

With a little practice, you'll taste the trend:

Warm climate = more ripe fruit, less acid
Cool climate = less ripe fruit, more acid

Another way of framing the same sense is Old World—meaning Europe—versus New World, meaning everywhere else. New World wines have a more overt fruitiness and sometimes sweetness. In wines from the Old World, flavors other than fruit—such as minerals, sea air, earth, or herbs—can dominate.

Getting to know specific grape varieties also helps. For example, if a red wine exhibits ripe cherry flavors, licorice, and minerals with low acidity and high alcohol, chances are you're tasting a warm-climate, Old World wine. Knowing that Garnacha exhibits ripe cherry and licorice notes, you can narrow your choices to where it grows in Southern Europe, such as the Southern Rhône Valley in France or in Spain.

GRAPES

Fruit is the first ingredient of wine. The species and variety of grape or grapes dramatically influence the style and flavor of a wine. Most of the time white grapes make white wine and red grapes make red wine—but what about pink? Do pink grapes exist?

Yes, some grape varieties have pink skins, but the lion's share of pink wine comes from a single variety of red grapes, followed by blends of red grapes or blends of red and white grapes.

Pink Grapes

The skin of the Pinot Gris grape—Pinot Grigio in Italy—has a pink tint. When the skins macerate, or steep, with the juice and/or wine, the skins' color transfers

TWO WORDS ON TERMINOLOGY

You may have heard the word "varietal," which many people—even longtime members of the wine trade—often misuse. In scientific taxonomy, as you'll recall from biology class, every living thing has a certain rank that goes from generic to specific: Domain, Kingdom, Phylum, Class, Order, Family, Genus, Species, and Variety. Most wine grapes belong to the following taxonomy: Eukaryota, Plantae, Angiosperms / Eudicots / Rosids, Vitales, Vitaceae, Vitis, vinifera.

Within the *Vitis vinifera* species, you'll find thousands of varieties, such as Cabernet Sauvignon, Merlot, Pinot Noir, and Syrah (all red); Chardonnay, Riesling, Sauvignon Blanc, and Sémillon (all white). Cabernet Sauvignon is a grape variety *not* a varietal. "Varietal" is an adjective that describes a wine made with only one variety of grape.

Also, *rosé* is French for "pink." It's *rosado* in Spanish and Portuguese, *rosato* in Italian, and *roz* in Greek.

into the wine. Pink grapes result in a fleshy pink wine with peach and floral flavors. When made as a rosé, Pinot Gris has medium acidity, alcohol, body, and flavor intensity.

Red Grapes

Red grapes come in many different shades, and the acidity, body, and flavors of wines made from them vary greatly. All else being equal, red grapes with thin skins, such as Pinot Noir, tend to make paler rosés than thick-skinned ones, such as Syrah and Cabernet Sauvignon, which make darker rosés. Below you'll find a list of red grapes commonly made as varietal wines, listed from thin-skinned with lighter, red fruit flavors at the top to thick-skinned with fuller body and black fruit flavors at the bottom.

PINOT NOIR Originally from Burgundy in France, this high-acid grape has flavors of light red berries, such as strawberry, cranberry, and red cherry.

GAMAY Also from France, this grape famously makes Beaujolais as well as light rosés with similar light red berry flavors as Pinot Noir but with lower acid, so it tastes less crisp or tart.

SANGIOVESE This grape makes the famous red wine of Chianti in Italy. It has high acidity, but it grows in warmer temperatures so has a little more color, weight, and alcohol than Pinot Noir and Gamay yet with similar flavors that fall within the red fruit family, such as cherry. You'll also taste a touch of herbs, such as oregano.

NERELLO MASCALESE This grape hails from Sicily. DNA research suggests that it might have a link to Sangiovese, and when tasting rosatos made from it you'll understand why. It has crisp acidity with flavors in the red fruit family.

MONTEPULCIANO Famous in Abruzzo, Italy, this red grape has a similar structure—body, acid, alcohol—and plenty of red berry flavors, but, on the scale, it's starting to slide into black fruit, such as blackberry and plum. It also has less acidity, which makes it softer on the palate.

GRENACHE Known as Garnacha in Spain, where it originated, this grape is a beach bunny. It loves sun and warm climates. In hot temperatures, the grape can generate a lot of sugar, which makes for a wine with high alcohol and full body. Wine made from it looks more orange-red than true red because it oxidizes (turning brown) easily. It tends to have low acid, and the flavors fall solidly in the red fruit family, specifically red cherry and raspberry for rosado wines. It also can have some black licorice flavor notes in the background.

TEMPRANILLO Another Spanish grape—and the predominant variety in the famous red wine of Rioja—it appears darker than Garnacha and has a bit higher acidity but not as much as Pinot Noir or the Italian grapes. You'll find red fruit flavors in rosados made from it but also some darker fruits, such as black cherry and blackberry.

CABERNET FRANC Rarely made into a varietal wine, this French variety often plays an important role in red blends, but winemakers in the Loire Valley do make it into a varietal rosé. You probably know it better as one of the parents of Cabernet Sauvignon, and you can taste the family resemblance in the black currant and herbal character of the wine. Rosés made from Cabernet Franc often have notes of raspberry and cherry, can taste very crisp, and come in a variety of styles (none as big as red or rosé wines made from Cabernet Sauvignon).

SYRAH Called Shiraz in Australia and South Africa, this grape makes red and rosé wines with a strong raspberry flavor, moderately full body, fairly warm alcohol, medium acidity, and some notes of black pepper. Shiraz rosés usually have stronger, more opulent fruit.

MERLOT Named for the blackbirds (*merles*) in Bordeaux that ate the fruit from the vines, Merlot grapes have thick skins and plummy black flavors with notes of black tea leaves in the finish. They can make a variety of styles in red wine, as well as rosés, depending on origin and winemaking methods.

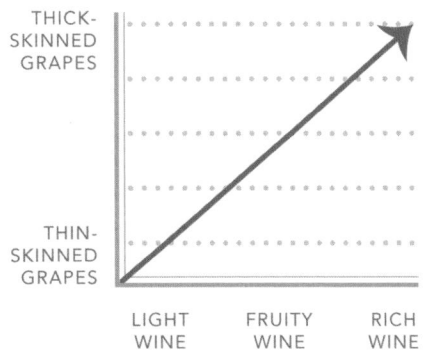

ZINFANDEL White Zinfandel isn't a grape; it's a wine made from the red Zinfandel grape and almost always made in a sweet style. Soaking the grape skins with the fermenting juice for a few hours creates that distinctive pink color.

MALBEC This grape originated in France but has found new life in South America. Like Merlot, it can make dark, deep, soft wines with plummy, blackberry flavors and hints of violet. Rosés made from it fall on the richer end of the spectrum with similar flavors, though not as intense as with red wines.

MOURVÈDRE Called Monastrell in Spain, it's the third most important red grape variety grown in that country. In Australia and California, it was and still is called Mataró. Whatever you call it, the grape makes deep, dark, blackberry-flavored wines that smell woodsy. The same applies to rosés made from it, which also appear darker than other thin-skinned varieties.

NEGROAMARO Literally "black-bitter" in Italian, this grape grows in southern Italy and makes dark, deep red wines. Rosatos made from it taste friendly and fruity, with red and black fruit flavors.

MENCIA This grape also comes from Spain and makes rich, brooding, dark red wines that can taste almost like Malbec with blackberry and violet flavors. A thick-skinned grape, it tends to create bold, rich rosados with blackberry, floral, and spicy flavors.

AGIORGITIKO The name of this grape, which hails from Greece, looks harder to pronounce than it is (page 163). It makes deep, dark reds with red and black fruit and fruity, full-bodied, bold rozes.

CABERNET SAUVIGNON Abbreviated by most people to "Cab," this French grape (a cross between Cabernet Franc and Sauvignon Blanc) originated in the fields of Bordeaux. It creates rich, dark reds with full body, richness, and intense black currant aromas. As a varietal rosé, it comes in a wide variety of styles from fully fruity to bold and rich.

BLENDS

It's important to know varietal rosés, but most are blends. Winemakers create blends for a number of reasons, including to:

* MAKE USE OF AVAILABLE GRAPES Sometimes you must use what nature gives you.
* GAIN COLOR In blends, some thin-skinned varieties appear pale, and a winemaker may add a thick-skinned variety to deepen the color of the final wine.
* GAIN ACIDITY As a varietal, some grapes have low acid and therefore taste overly fruity, but, when blended with a grape higher in acid, the final wine has better balance. Chardonnay, for example, often goes into rosé champagnes for its light body and higher acidity.
* REDUCE BITTERNESS Some grapes as a varietal can taste bitter, but blending them with a softer grape variety—red or white—can reduce the tannic bitterness in the final wine. For example, as you'll see in the Rich chapter (p. 133), a predominantly Cabernet Sauvignon–based blend has 15 percent Viognier, a white grape, to soften the edges of the thick-skinned, tannic Cab grape.

* CREATE DIFFERENT FLAVORS Winemakers create blends much like chefs use different spices in cooking. In the Southern Rhône in France, for example, winemakers often blend Mourvèdre with Grenache to improve the structure of and add depth of flavor to their rosés.

WINEMAKING

After harvest, the winemaker controls the final style and flavor of a wine. With rosé, it depends on how the juice releases from the grapes, how long the skins sit in the juice and/or wine, the temperature before and during fermentation, and whether or how the winemaker blends wines before bottling. The different methods often represent the traditions of a particular region that might have changed over time.

Direct Press

Provençal winemakers employ this method, which uses red grapes with white wine production methods. The red grapes come into the winery, go through a destemming machine, and then are crushed to create a mixture of juice, pulp, seeds, and skins, a mixture known as "must." The must is pressed immediately, then placed into the fermentation tank. The skins have contact with the juice for a very short period of time, which explains why the resulting wine appears pale.

Pre-fermentation Maceration

Many New World winemakers use this method for rosé wines. Also known as *macération pélliculaire*, skin contact is when the grape skins have a pre-fermentation soak in the must for a few hours or sometimes a few days. The color from the red skins darkens the must sort of like tea: the longer it steeps, the darker it gets. This method creates darker wine than with the direct press method. If the temperature during pre-fermentation maceration is cold (53–59°F), it's called a cold soak

and retains more fruity aromas. A higher temperature before fermentation results in lower fruitiness. The extended time on the skins also increases the pH, lowering acidity and concentrating amino acids, which makes for a more predictable and better fermentation. The resulting wine appears

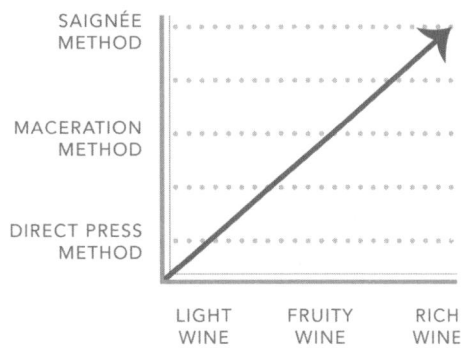

deeper in color, and has more intense fruit flavors and generally more weight than wines made with the direct press method.

Winemakers can't use this method everywhere, though. In some hot, dry climates, some red grapes create too many phenolic compounds—chemicals responsible for the color and bitterness in red wine—resulting in a rosé with too much bitterness or astringency.

Saignée

In this method, which means "bled" in French, the winemaker draws liquid from the must while red wine is fermenting in the fermentation tank. As must creates wine, the alcohol level increases. Alcohol is an extracting agent, so as it increases it draws more color and flavor from the skins, resulting in a more deeply colored wine than by the direct press method and cold-soak method.

Winemakers in Spain and Italy often use the saignée method. In Spain, wine made this way is called *vino clarete*, and skin contact during fermentation takes place for only a short time. In Italy, it's called *chiaretto* and used occasionally for darker rosés.

In Bordeaux, winemakers call this style *clairet*, which, according to Oz Clarke, gave Bordeaux wine its famous nickname of "claret" centuries ago.

Blending

Winemakers use this method to make rosé champagne. They make the champagne (page 31), then add a small amount of red wine before bottling to create the desired shade of pink—and voilà: rosé champagne. This method allows for consistent color, year after year, which matters for champagne, which predominantly contains a blend of vintages to maintain a traditional house style. Consistency counts!

BLENDING CONTROVERSY

Though allowed for making rosé champagne, traditionally it has been illegal in France to blend red and white wines together. Outrage erupted in 2009 when EU agriculture commissioner Mariann Fischer Boel proposed allowing the blending of red and white wines to compete more effectively with New World rosés.

"The battle for rosé's nobility risks being lost with a wave of Europe's magic wand," said Xavier de Volontat, president of the AGPV, the French union of wine producers, adding that it would lead to economic and social destruction.

Why the apocalyptic controversy? Protectionism, on the one hand. Many Europeans want to maintain their defining traditions—which make for some subtle, high-quality rosés—to distinguish their ways, by law, from New World production methods. On the other hand, some people just want to turn a quick profit, traditions be damned, which runs the risk of flooding the market with otherwise unsellable white wine doctored with a little red to make it pink.

Cofermentation

It's still illegal to blend red wine with white to make rosé in France—again, except champagne—but winemakers have found loopholes. French law says nothing about cofermenting red and white grapes together, which winemakers do for *vin gris* in France and *claretes* in Spain. Spanish winemakers always make *claretes* by cofermenting red and white grapes, traditionally Garnacha and Viura, and then using the saignée method.

Nor does French law have a problem with blending within the same category, meaning blending lighter rosé must/wine with darker rosé must/wine. The first extraction happens between 12 and 36 hours for the first pink must, and the second happens later for a deeper rosé must. Tavel winemakers in the Côtes du Rhône generally create their rosés this way, resulting in that beautiful deep color and rich flavor profile.

SPARKLING ROSÉ

All sparkling wines, regardless of their final color, begin life as plain old wine. The equation for making all wines is

$$\text{Sugar} + \text{yeast} = \text{alcohol} + \text{carbon dioxide}$$

but with still wines the carbon dioxide evaporates. Sparkling wines create and capture a second set of carbon dioxide bubbles through various methods, usually a second fermentation. The techniques of confining the bubbles vary and, no surprise, can have a profound impact on a wine's structure.

TRADITIONAL METHOD Called *méthode Champenoise* in champagne only, *méthode traditionelle* or *classique* elsewhere in France, and *método tradicional* in Spain for cava, this is the method used in champagne and for champagne-style sparkling wines. The second fermentation takes place in the bottle itself. Winemakers add sugar and yeast to the base wine and seal it with a temporary cap, which traps the new carbon dioxide inside the bottle. The longer the wine stays in the bottle, the smaller the bubbles become. For non-vintage champagne, the minimum is 15 months, and two years for vintage champagnes. The smallest bubbles create the finest texture, resulting in the highest-quality sparklers.

CHARMAT METHOD The second fermentation for this method takes place in giant steel vats, which trap the carbon dioxide and force it into the wine. This technique creates larger bubbles than the traditional method but smaller than with carbonation. Winemakers can create extremely large volumes of sparkling

32

wine this way, which allows them to market the final wines at more affordable price points. Most Prosecco is made this way.

CARBONATION METHOD Just as with soda, winemakers inject the base wine with carbon dioxide gas under high pressure. The resulting bubbles are quite large and don't last as long as other methods, but it gets the job done.

SWEETNESS

We'll look at sweetness as a function of taste in more detail in the next chapter, but the winemaking process also determines the final sweetness of a wine. Different countries and regions have different names and rules for various levels of sweetness, but for rosés the three general levels, in ascending order, are off-dry, semi-sweet, and sweet. Winemakers can employ three primary techniques to create sweet wines:

FILTER YEAST Removing the yeast halts the fermentation process and preserves some of the original sugar content. This method also creates low-alcohol wines.

ADD SUGAR A winemaker can add sugar or unfermented grape juice for sweetness but only after fermentation; otherwise it turns into alcohol.

ADD ALCOHOL Alcohol kills yeast, so for a higher-alcohol wine a winemaker can add brandy (distilled wine) before fermentation finishes, thereby killing the yeast, preserving the residual sugar, and increasing the alcohol level.

If a wine contains residual sugar, winemakers must add an antimicrobial agent, such as sulfur dioxide, to prevent spoilage; otherwise an additional fermentation can create unintentional bubbles or flavors. Drinker beware: if you have a sensitivity or allergy to sulfur dioxide, you should avoid wines that contain sulfur dioxide.

2

TASTING
⇒ ROSÉ ⇐

Your sense of smell is one of the most important tools when tasting wine, because most of what you perceive as flavors are actually aromas. Your sense of smell represents about 90 percent of your sense of taste. (That other 10 percent is flavor.)

Don't believe me? Think back to the last time you had a cold or bad allergy attack. You couldn't breathe through your stuffy nose, which made everything you ate or drank taste bland, right? When your nasal passages become congested, that obstruction prevents you from perceiving aroma *as well as* taste.

The Nose Knows

Your sense of smell matters more than you might think. Smelling gas or smoke can alert you to invisible dangers. You recoil when food spoils because it smells rotten, saving you from sickness. Scientists have noted the relationship between smell and choosing a mate: the better your mate smells to you, the more likely that you have complementary immune systems, maximizing the ability of your offspring to fight infection.

When you smell wine, aromatic compounds travel up your nose and reach chemical receptors in your nasal cavity. Those receptors send signals to the olfactory bulb, which tells your brain what you're smelling. You can also smell flavors after you've swallowed something. After you swallow, aromas don't travel through your nose but behind your tongue, through your retronasal cavity, to those same receptors. That's why, after burping, you sometimes taste something you ate hours earlier.

But not everyone smells alike. I've spent years fine-tuning my sense of smell, but I don't get some aromas that some people identify in some wines. Fellow experts say that Grüner Veltliner, an Austrian white, smells of lentils, but I've never detected that smell in any Grüner I've tasted. Does that make my palate somehow deficient? No, it just means that I don't smell lentils in Grüner Veltliner—and that's okay.

When starting to appreciate wine, most people have problems identifying what their palates are telling them, and that's because we don't practice our sense of smell the same way we practice our sense of sight or touch. Let's use an analogy with a box of crayons. Your first box of crayons probably had just eight colors in it. That's fine at first, but then you got the 16-count and then the 32-count box of crayons, which not only has red and orange crayons but a crayon called "red-orange" that's a different hue from "orange-red." The 64-crayon box has blue and green crayons as well as royal blue, teal, turquoise, aquamarine, and periwinkle. Each has its own distinctive color. You can distinguish between teal and royal blue easily now because you practiced your sense of sight with those crayons.

Thankfully, you also can practice your sense of smell.

Four Ways to Improve Your Sense of Smell

The easiest way to sharpen your olfactory receptors is to pay close attention to the aromas all around you. Make mental or written notes of different smells and flavors whenever you eat.

Next, you can go to your kitchen cabinet or spice rack and practice honing your scent sense with what you already own: cinnamon, nutmeg, rosemary, walnuts, and so on.

Then, go to the supermarket and buy foods typically mentioned in wine tasting notes: apricot, blackberry, cherry (red and black), lemon, lime, nectarine, passion fruit, peach, raspberry, and strawberry. Cut them open, smell them, taste them, and make a mental note of how each smells and tastes.

Many wine books have a wheel or table of aromas and flavors that you can study, which helps at the advanced level, but the comprehensive ones can look a bit intimidating at first because they include obscure scents as well as unpleasant aromas for identifying faults in bad wine. Rather than give you a dizzying wheel or an overwhelming table, here are eight broad aroma categories along with some common sample descriptions:

FRUITY banana, cherry, lemon, peach, plum
FLORAL hibiscus, jasmine, lily, rose, violet
HERBAL eucalyptus, grass, lavender, mint, rosemary
EARTHY bread, forest floor, graphite, mushroom, stone
SPICY anise, black pepper, cinnamon, ginger, nutmeg
NUTTY almond, brazil nut, hazelnut, pecan, walnut
SWEET butterscotch, caramel, honey, molasses, vanilla
WOODY cedar, pine, smoke, toast, tobacco

Obviously not all of these will apply to rosé, but it's a good place to start if you're not sure how to identify what you're smelling and tasting.

However you go about refining your sense of smell, remember that the more you understand the different aromas you perceive, the more you'll enhance your overall experience with and enjoyment of wine.

Heed Your Tongue

Try this test. Pinch your nostrils shut, and eat a piece of chocolate. Not much flavor, is there? Let go of your nose before you finish the chocolate, however, and you'll experience a huge taste rush as you breathe in. Your nose can perceive approximately 200 compounds in wine, but your tongue can perceive just five tastes: sweet, sour, salty, umami, and bitter.

SWEET

Sweetness is easy to perceive, especially for us Americans. We love sugar. In wine, the opposite of sweet is dry, but people often confuse dry, sweet, and fruity—especially with rosés. Fruity is an aroma rather than a flavor. A fruity wine can taste bone-dry, while another wine can have a lot of sweetness but little fruit. For example, Mateus The Original and Broadbent Vinho Verde Rosé are sweet but have less fruit, while Carmel Road Barrymore Rosé of Pinot Noir and Raidis Cheeky Goat Pinot Gris are dry, fruit-forward wines.

Another mistake: we tend to equate dry wine with increased sophistication, yet some of the best wines in the world are sweet—Port, Sauternes, and Tokaji. There's nothing wrong with liking a sweet wine. It's a matter of personal preference. If you like sweet wine, embrace it with pride!

SOUR

Our brains register sourness when food or drink has high acidity. Have you ever bitten into a fresh lemon or a sour candy? Your mouth puckers, and the sides of your tongue tingle. That's acidity. It sounds unpleasant, but acidity serves two key functions in wine: it helps us perceive more flavors, and it helps the wine age longer. The next time you're cooking or making something with lemon juice, taste it before and after you add the ingredient. The acidity of the lemon juice stimulates your palate. Acidity is easier to perceive in dry wine. Conversely, the more sugar, the harder it is to sense the acidity. Some German Rieslings may seem low in acid because they're sweet, but they actually have high acidity levels. Acidity can take getting used to, but, in time, your palate will adapt and you'll be able to pick up more of the fruit and other flavors in the wine.

SALTY AND UMAMI

Salt is another easy one. When your tongue detects sodium ions, you perceive something as salty. The more sodium ions, the saltier the taste. Wine, however, doesn't contain salt. Other alkali metals can provide a salty taste, but the further they range from sodium on the periodic table, the less salty something will taste. Some wines, such as Muscadet and Fino Sherry, can have an aroma reminiscent of brine or salty almonds, but that's an aroma rather than a flavor, so that doesn't count.

Umami means "good flavor" or "good taste" in Japanese. Experts describe it as a brothy, meaty, or savory taste. Protein-rich foods—such as broth, cheese, meat, and stock—are high in umami. There's no umami in wine, either.

ACID HIGH

You may think you don't like high-acid beverages or foods, but if you like coffee, tomato sauce, yogurt, or corn, you like high acidity.

BITTER

Bitterness is the most sensitive of the tastes, and tannin represents the primary source of bitterness in wine. Tannin belongs to a chemical group called polyphenols. Some people use the two terms interchangeably, but tannin is a subset of polyphenols, and it comes from grape skins, seeds, stems, and oak barrels.

THE GRAPE TEST

Have you ever eaten red table grapes (which have seeds) and chewed on the skin or bitten into one of the seeds? If you haven't, try some. You'll understand firsthand how bitterness in the grape translates into the wine.

Red grapes have "black" flesh and white juice. To achieve those beautiful colors, the fermenting juice sits in the skins to draw the color from them. That process also extracts tannin and other polyphenols. Not surprisingly, red and rosé wines have more bitterness than white wines. You can perceive tannin, particularly in red wine, as a gripping or drying sensation in your mouth with bitterness in the aftertaste. Like acidity, many people find bitterness unpleasant, but it adds texture, makes a wine last longer, and provides certain health benefits. As with sweetness, people have varying thresholds for bitterness. A wine that tastes bitingly bitter to you may taste lusciously soft to someone else.

Alcohol

Remember your first sip of hard alcohol? A sensation like fire ran from your mouth down to your stomach and then back up again. We perceive alcohol as a heat sensation on our palates. Wines high in alcohol can taste "hot" in a similar way. We also can taste alcohol as bitterness or as a little sweetness. As we saw in the last chapter, the simple formula for making wine is:

$$Sugar + yeast = alcohol + carbon\ dioxide$$

The more sugar, the higher the alcohol level. Because some grape varieties have higher sugar contents than others, their wines wind up containing more alcohol. Some Garnachas can have alcohol levels of more than 15 percent. Geography plays a key role here as well. Take Chardonnay, for example. It grows in both cool and warm climates. Chardonnay from Chablis, a cool region in the north of France, generally has an alcohol level of around 12.5 percent, but Chardonnay grown in the sunny state of California can reach levels up to 14.5 percent or more.

MODERATE CONSUMPTION

The U.S. Department of Health standardizes one drink to mean 5 ounces of wine at about 12% ABV (alcohol by volume). Moderate consumption means one drink per day for women and no more than two for men, but moderation can vary based on a person's size. The more mass a person has, the less concentrated the alcohol will be in his or her system. Women also process alcohol differently than men because we generally have less muscle mass than men. It sounds unfair, but studies have shown that women also have a more developed sense of smell, so in a way it balances out. Additionally, five ounces isn't a standard portion for all wines. The higher the alcohol level, the less it takes to equal one standard drink. One glass of California Zinfandel at 14.8 percent has almost *twice* the alcohol of a German Riesling at 8 percent.

THE FIVE Ss

There is a proper way to taste wine. It may look like showing off or indulging in wine snobbery, but each step has a particular purpose. The five *Ss* are:

1. See
2. Swirl
3. Sniff
4. Sip
5. Savor

Put them all together, and you'll maximize your enjoyment of your next glass of wine.

HOW TO HOLD A GLASS PROPERLY

Before we take a closer look at each step—so you can determine a wine's quality and get the most from every sip—we need to review one quick fundamental. If a glass has a stem, that's what you're supposed to hold. Think of it like a coffee cup: the cup has a handle to separate your point of contact from the part of the vessel containing the liquid. The same goes for a wineglass. Never hold the glass by the bowl. Why not? The temperature of your hand changes the wine. Warm wine tastes less fruity, and your palate will focus on the alcohol instead. Alcohol compounds release more quickly at warmer temperatures, so the wine will taste more alcoholic and therefore more bitter. Holding the glass by the stem allows the wine to remain at a more constant temperature so you can enjoy it longer.

See

A wine's color can tell you a lot about how it will taste, its richness, condition, and likely aromas and flavors. The best way to examine the color is to tilt the glass over a white surface, such as a white table cloth or a white napkin. Doing this will give you its true color. Wine in the meniscus, or center, of the glass sometimes appears the same as and sometimes different from wine at the edge or rim. Thick-skinned grapes, such as Cabernet Sauvignon, make for deeper wine, while thin-skinned varieties, such as Pinot Noir, look much paler in the glass. Generally speaking, the deeper the color, the higher the tannins. Young wines tend to have a brighter color, but all wines change color as they age. White wines gain color, while red wines lose it. In both categories, over time, wine tends toward brownish orange hues. A brownish color also indicates oxidation.

Swirl

Swirling may look showy, but it has an important purpose. Some of the aroma compounds in wine are more or less stable than others. The volatile or less stable ones release into the air more easily. In either case, the compounds must travel through the air and into your nose for you to be able to detect them. Swirling achieves this aim. If the thought of swirling the glass while holding the stem makes you nervous, place the glass on a table for stability and move the foot of the glass in a circular motion.

Sniff

There are different ways to smell a wine, depending on its style. For a rich or heavy one, I recommend the Chest, Chin, Nose approach. For a lighter, more delicate wine, skip chest and chin and go right to nose.

First hold the wine at chest level. You can smell aromatic grape varieties, such as Muscat, at this level. The compounds you detect here have the most volatility, so these aromas will differ from those at your chin and nose. Often these aromas are the most fruity.

Now hold the glass to your chin and smell again. You'll sense much more intense fruit here, but you also may be able to pick up other types of aromas, perhaps floral, herbal, or nutty notes.

Finally, stick your nose in the glass—literally. Stick it all the way inside, and take a big whiff. Pull the glass away, then do it again twice more. Try different smell tactics to determine what works best for your nose. Maybe one nostril is more perceptive than the other, in which case tilt your head. Maybe you get more sensory information from a series of short sniffs rather than one long inhalation.

You've probably heard people comment on the complexity of a wine. You may not smell many layers of aromas right away, but that's okay. Take the time to heed what your nose is telling you. The more you pay attention, the more you'll enjoy.

Sip

You need enough wine in your mouth for your taste buds to perceive all the flavors. Take in about a tablespoonful, and roll it around your tongue. This action aerates the wine, warms it up, and releases aromatic compounds. Note the weight and texture of the wine in your mouth. If that sounds perplexing, think about the differences among skim milk, whole milk, and heavy cream. Some wines are light and delicate, while others feel heavy and dense. Slurp some air over the top of the wine in your mouth to aerate the wine even more. It may look and sound silly, but professional wine tasters do it this way because it releases the maximum aromas and flavors.

Savor

This is the time to reflect on what you've just tasted. Think about the wine and whether you like it, keeping in mind the difference between preference and quality. Sometimes they're the same, sometimes not. Savoring allows you to decipher between the two. Three parameters can help you determine a wine's quality level.

COMPLEXITY is like an ice cream sundae. You start with vanilla ice cream. Now add hot fudge. Do you like it less or more? Layer it with toasted nuts and peanut butter chips. How about now? Finish it with whipped cream and a cherry. The same principle holds true for wine. When a wine has many layers, we call it complex. If all you taste is fruit and nothing else, it's a simple or one-dimensional wine. More layers or complexity indicates that a wine has higher quality. Keep in mind, though, that the layers should complement one another. You certainly wouldn't want tomato sauce on your ice cream sundae!

BALANCE happens in wine when all components—acidity, alcohol, fruit, tannin, and weight—interact in harmony, like a symphony. If the horns overpower the violins or you can't hear the percussionists at all, it sounds disconnected. When an orchestra plays in balance, no single instrument stands out. The same holds true for wine. Sometimes one element does stand out, though. Wines from hot climates can have very high alcohol levels, for example. That's fine if the other components balance it accordingly, but if all you taste is boozy bitterness then the wine has lost its balance.

LENGTH in wine is the time that the taste remains in your mouth, and that amount varies from person to person. If a wine lasts a long time—say, a minute or more—it has long length, which indicates higher quality. Remember, though, that it should taste pleasant, not flawed!

PREFERENCE VS. QUALITY

Let's say you don't like oaked Chardonnays, but you try one and notice that the complexity and balance last a long time. That tells you that it's a good-quality wine. You might not prefer the style or taste, and, again, that's okay.

COMPONENT TASTING

If you're really serious about improving your palate and your perception of acidity, alcohol, sweetness, and tannin, try this component tasting, which will help you isolate those elements of a wine in the glass. You'll need:

* 1 bottle Italian Pinot Grigio
* 5 wineglasses, all the same type
* measuring cup and spoons
* eyedropper
* dry-erase marker or sticky notes and a pen or pencil
* lemon juice
* vodka
* sugar
* wine tannin powder or cinnamon
* glass of water

Italian Pinot Grigio is fairly easy to find and more or less consistent across the board: it has medium body, medium alcohol, medium fruit intensity, medium acid, and no tannins. You can buy wine tannin powder at any homebrewing or wine-making store or online. If you can't find it, use cinnamon, which has a high level of tannin, but then disregard the aroma and focus on the texture.

Place all five wineglasses in a row in front of you. Number each glass either with the marker on the base of each glass or with sticky notes in front of each glass. Open the wine and measure out four ounces into each of the five glasses. (You'll still have some wine left in the bottle if you mess up.)

GLASS 1 This is your control glass for comparisons. Don't add anything to it.

GLASS 2 Add two or three drops of lemon juice and swirl the glass or stir. This will increase the acidity level. Compare with the control glass, then take a sip of water to clear your palate. If you can't taste the difference against the control glass, add a few more drops of lemon juice.

GLASS 3 Add a few drops of vodka and swirl or stir. This will increase the alcohol level. Compare with the control glass, then take a sip of water to clear your palate. As with the lemon juice, if you can't taste the difference against the control glass, add a few more drops.

GLASS 4 Add ¼ teaspoon sugar and swirl or stir until it dissolves. This will raise the sweetness level. Compare with the control glass, then take a sip of water to clear your palate. Again, if you can't taste the difference against the control glass, add a little more until you can.

GLASS 5 Add a pinch of wine tannin powder and stir. The wine will go brown, but that's okay because we're focusing on taste rather than color. Note the drying sensation on your palate. Compare with the control glass, then take a sip of water to clear your palate.

3

THE
⇒ ROSÉ QUIZ & ⇐
WHEEL

This quick ten-question quiz will help you identify rosés that you'll enjoy, and it also can help you select wines for your colleagues, friends, loved ones, and others. Each answer you provide generates a point score that you'll record in the tally column on the right. Don't think about the answers too much. Go with your gut instinct rather than agonizing over each question. At the end of the quiz, total your score, then use the answer key to find your personal preference in one of four categories: Blush, Crisp, Fruity, and Rich.

THE ROSÉ QUIZ

Question		3 Points	
1.	How do you drink your coffee or tea?	black / plain	
2.	How much sugar or sweetener do you add to your coffee or tea?	none	
3.	What type of chocolate do you prefer?	dark chocolate	
4.	How often do you put lemon juice on your fish, chicken, or green beans?	never	
5.	What's your favorite juice?	I don't drink juice, too sweet.	
6.	How spicy do you like your food?	extremely hot	
7.	What kind of milk do you like to drink?	whole	
8.	What type of perfume or cologne do you like most?	spicy or intense	
9.	What flavor of gum do you prefer?	cinnamon	
10.	What's your favorite kind of snack?	something rich: chocolate or fudge	

2 Points	1 Point	0 Points	TOTAL
a little milk or cream	a lot of milk or cream	I don't drink coffee or tea.	
just a dash	2 packets	I like it really sweet.	
milk chocolate	white chocolate	I don't eat or like chocolate.	
sometimes	always	not sure	
lemonade or cranberry juice	orange or apple juice	grape juice, fruit punch, juice drinks	
medium	mild	not at all	
2 percent	skim	not sure	
fruity	floral or fresh	sweet or candied	
cherry, grape, watermelon	spearmint, peppermint, wintergreen	bubblegum	
fruit or something with fruit in it: apple, banana, orange, dried fruit, fruit yogurt	something salty: chips, nuts, pretzels	candy: hard candy, red licorice, jelly beans	

BLUSH 1–13 points
CRISP 14–19 points
FRUITY 20–25 points
RICH 26–33 points

The Rosé Quiz & Wheel

Once you know your category, go to the Rosé Wheel to see which wines fit your profile.

If you want to cut to the chase, hit the wine store with that list of wines that will please your palate. No stressful memorizing, no lengthy explanations. It's that easy!

If you want to know more, however, keep reading this chapter to understand how the quiz works. You'll also find helpful hints if your results don't align with your known preferences.

THE ROSÉ WHEEL

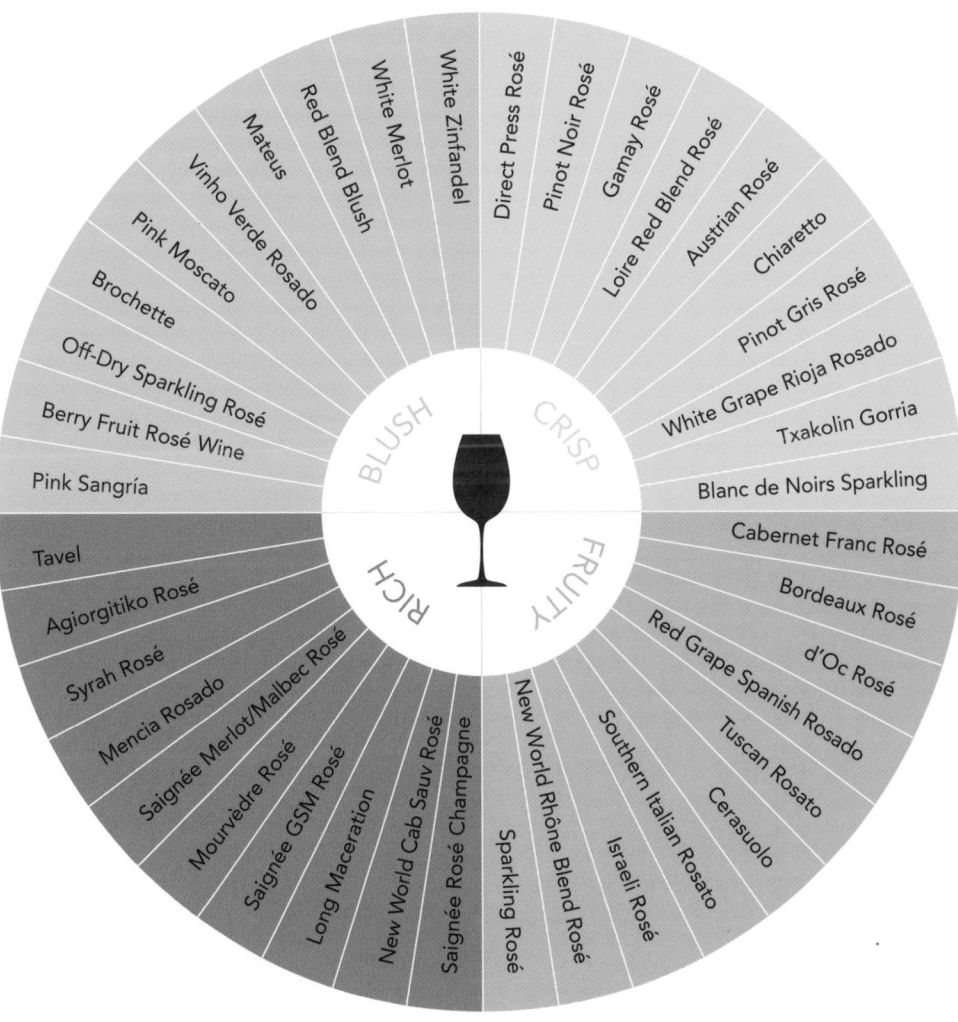

Blush Style

1. White Zinfandel
2. White Merlot
3. Red Blend Blush
4. Mateus
5. Vinho Verde Rosado
6. Pink Moscato
7. Brochette
8. Off-Dry Sparkling Rosé
9. Berry Fruit Rosé Wine
10. Pink Sangria

Fruity

1. Cabernet Franc Rosé
2. Bordeaux Rosé
3. d'Oc Rosé
4. Red Grape Spanish Rosado
5. Tuscan Rosato
6. Cerasuolo
7. Southern Italian Rosato
8. Israeli Rosé
9. New World Rhône Blend Rosé
10. Sparkling Rosé

Crisp Style

1. Direct Press Rosé
2. Pinot Noir Rosé
3. Gamay Rosé
4. Loire Red Blend Rosé
5. Austrian Rosé
6. Chiaretto
7. Pinot Gris Rosé
8. Whit Grape Rioja Rosado
9. Txakolin Gorria
10. Blanc de Noirs Sparkling

Rich Style

1. Tavel
2. Agiorgitiko Rose
3. Syrah Rosé
4. Mencia Rosado
5. Saignée Merlot and Malbec Rosé
6. Mourvèdre Rosé
7. Saignée GSM Rosé
8. Long Maceration
9. New World Cabernet Sauvignon Rosé
10. Saignée Rosé Champagne

Rosé Style Characteristics

BLUSH

Color, flavor, and fruit concentration may vary, but all blush wines taste sweet. If you fall into the blush category, other wines will taste too bitter or sour for you. Characteristics include:

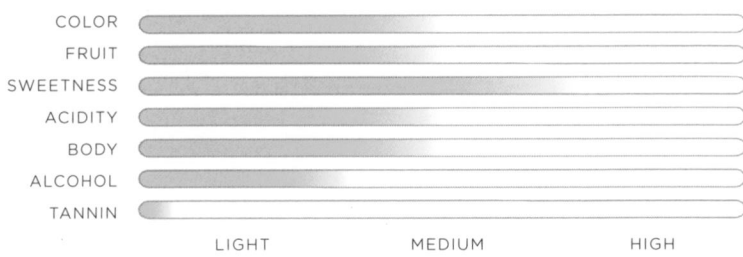

CRISP

These delicate wines have a lot of acidity, which makes them refreshing, particularly in the heat. Their soft aromas often feature floral, herbal, or mineral notes. Characteristics include:

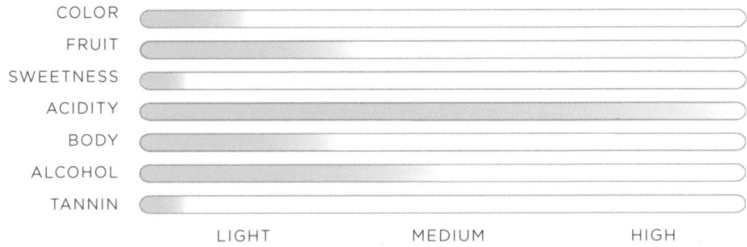

FRUITY

Like the Crisp category, these wines can feature floral and herbal aroma and flavor notes, but the fruit stands clearly above the rest.

Characteristics include:

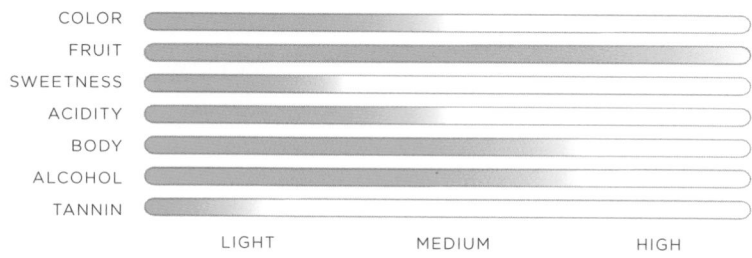

RICH

These are big, bold, lush, powerful, rich wines. In some cases, they can taste like light reds.

Characteristics include:

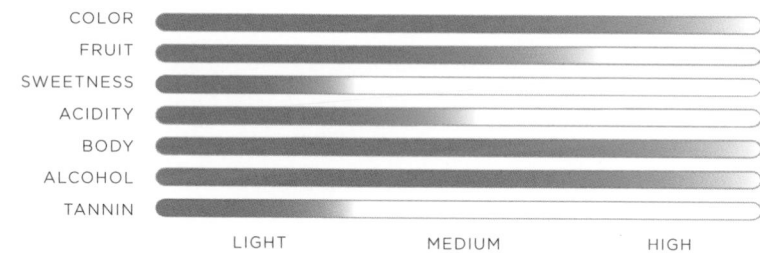

How the Rosé Quiz Works

The ten questions of the Rosé Quiz don't ask anything specifically about wine, but each question targets your palate's reaction to one or more element of wine. Let's break down each question to see what it reveals.

1. HOW DO YOU DRINK YOUR COFFEE OR TEA?

This question determines your tolerance for bitterness. Coffee and tea contain tannin, which creates a drying, astringent, sometimes bitter sensation in the mouth. If you add milk, a chemical reaction occurs between the protein in the milk and the tannin, which softens the overall drink on your palate. If you take your coffee black or your tea plain, you have a high tolerance for bitterness and therefore tannin. Some red wines have a lot of tannin, as do some rosés. Blush drinkers have the lowest tolerance for bitterness and add the most milk or cream to cut the bitterness. Crisp and Fruity lie in the middle, and, at the opposite end, Rich drinkers take their coffee or tea black or plain. Few wines if any taste bitter to them.

2. HOW MUCH SUGAR OR SWEETENER DO YOU ADD TO YOUR COFFEE OR TEA?

This question determines your tolerance for bitterness and sweetness together. Sugar doesn't react chemically with tannins the way milk does, but it does mask bitterness by distracting your palate. Blush rosés taste sweet by definition. The other categories are dry. Unsurprisingly, the Blush style appeals to those with a higher tolerance for sweet beverages. That doesn't mean that if you like Blush rosés you won't like any other styles. You might like dry, fruity wines. But the lower your score, the more likely your taste buds prefer sweet over bitter.

3. WHAT TYPE OF CHOCOLATE DO YOU PREFER?

This question also determines your tolerance for bitterness and sweetness together. The level of cacao in chocolate establishes its bitterness. (If you've ever eaten bitter baking chocolate, you know what I mean!) Dark chocolate, like baking chocolate, has more cacao in it, imparting more bitterness and less sweetness. Blush drinkers don't like dark or even semisweet chocolate because it tastes too bitter. Rich drinkers, on the other hand, have a high tolerance for bitterness and prefer dark chocolate. That doesn't make milk chocolate the middle of the road, though. Milk chocolate has less cacao but lots of sugar to mask the bitterness, so this question, as with the sweetness of your coffee or tea, determines your threshold for bitterness and sweetness together. If you like sweet wine, you might like milk chocolate, but that may have more to do with the sugar content than the cacao percentage. White chocolate—all cocoa butter and no cacao, so technically not chocolate—appeals most to Blush drinkers.

4. HOW OFTEN DO YOU PUT LEMON ON YOUR FISH, CHICKEN, OR GREEN BEANS?

This question determines your tolerance for acidity. Lemon juice has a lot of acid; some people like that, others not so much. Wine has varying levels of acidity.

Some grapes and wine styles can taste almost electric, while others feel much softer. Crisp rosés are the most acidic. When you apply acidity to food, you make a dish's flavors pop, which makes Crisp rosés extremely food-friendly.

5. WHAT'S YOUR FAVORITE JUICE?

This question determines your tolerance for acidity and sweetness together. Citrus juices generally have the highest acidity. If you prefer lemonade or cranberry juice, you have a high tolerance for tartness and acidity, pushing you into the Crisp category. But, as before, sugar can distract your palate, so this question helps quantify whether you like acidity or dislike sweetness. If you like juices that taste more like candy, you're a Blush drinker. If you like strong fruit flavors, Fruity rosés are more your style. Rich drinkers can appreciate the intensity and concentration of fruit juice but generally dislike their sweetness.

6. HOW SPICY DO YOU LIKE YOUR FOOD?

This question determines your tolerance for alcohol. Alcohol has a thermal reaction in your mouth, creating a heat sensation, which makes wine taste "hot." The same reaction happens with spice. If you've ever had a bite of something incredibly spicy, you know what I mean. Your mouth feels like it's burning, you start to sweat, your eyes water. If you don't like spice, chances are you won't like high-alcohol wines. On the other end of the spectrum, if your motto is "The hotter the better!" then you'll enjoy the boozier bottles.

7. WHAT KIND OF MILK DO YOU LIKE TO DRINK?

This question determines your preference for body. Drinking milk obviously isn't the same as drinking wine, but this question isolates how you feel about the weight and texture of the liquid, which can be hard to consider abstractly. Climate, grape variety, and winemaking style can impact a wine's weight. This question helps narrow those fields.

8. WHAT TYPE OF PERFUME OR COLOGNE DO YOU LIKE MOST?

This question establishes what aromas you like. You shouldn't drink perfume or cologne, but you should smell wine. Most perfumes and colognes combine different categories of scents—sweet, candied, floral, fruity, spicy, intense—but many of them have a dominant top note category. For example, Estée Lauder Pleasures perfume contains many floral aromas, such as lily, peony, jasmine, and Baie rose. The same goes for Issey Miyake, also a very floral perfume. On the other end of the spectrum, Opium by Yves St. Laurent has some floral notes, but exotic spices dominate: clove, coriander, myrrh, cedar, and sandalwood.

Colognes generally smell more intense and spicy and feature scents of bergamot, cardamom, cedar, and musk. But some smell more aquatic and fresh, such as Davidoff Cool Water; sweet, such as Ralph Lauren Polo Black; or spicy, like Calvin Klein Obsession.

Sweet perfumes tend to smell like candy, such as Viktor & Rolf's Flower Bomb, Pink Sugar by Aqualina, and DKNY's Pink Macaroon.

A MATTER OF TASTE

Don't worry if there's a disconnect between the scents you like to wear and what you like to drink. You might like spicy, intense smells, but not spicy food or rich rosés. That's a great example of the important difference between aroma and flavor.

9. WHAT FLAVOR OF GUM DO YOU PREFER?

This question determines what flavors you like. If you like cinnamon gum, you have a high tolerance for spice. If you like fruity gum, then of course you like fruity flavors. If you go for the spearmint family in chewing gum, you probably prefer Crisp rosés. If sweet bubblegum is your style, then you'll enjoy Blush wines.

10. WHAT'S YOUR FAVORITE SNACK?

This question determines what overall tastes you like, and it helps solidify which category fits you best. Some blush wines taste like liquid candy. You can practically taste the saltiness of sea air in a glass of Provençal rosé. If, when hunger strikes, your first instinct is to reach for the fruit bowl, then fruity rosés will suit you best. Chocoholics tend to fall into the Rich category.

Frequently Asked Questions

Now that you understand how the quiz works and what it reveals about your palate preferences, you may still have some questions. These are the most common.

CAN I CHANGE MY ANSWERS?

Of course. Now that you know the reasoning behind the questions, you might want to rethink some of your answers. Feel free to go back and recalculate. The point is to find out what will appeal most to your palate!

IS THE ROSÉ QUIZ FOOLPROOF?

Of course not—but, like *Color Me Beautiful*, a 1980s makeup book that inspired my first book, *The One Minute Wine Master*, it will give you a starting point to feel comfortable and to explore the complex world of wine. This quiz uses averages, so if you like big, powerful rosés and blush wines, the quiz results might drop you perplexingly on the cusp between Crisp and Fruity. How can you tell? Take a closer look at your answers. If you like grape juice, sweet perfumes, fruity gum, fruit snacks, you'll probably enjoy fruity Blush rosés or Fruity rosés that are dry. Even if the quiz doesn't gauge you perfectly, the wheel still gives you a starting point for discovering new wines.

CAN MY CATEGORY CHANGE?

Absolutely—as your tastes evolve, so will your category. Our tastes change as we age and encounter new smells, flavors, tastes, and textures. Your category can change with the climate as well. As the weather cools, we gravitate to richer foods and wines. Conversely, during hot months, we eat lighter dishes and drink lighter wines. You may find that you enjoy Crisp wines in the summer and Rich rosés in the winter. Where you live also can influence what wine you prefer. When I lived in New York City, which has four distinct seasons, I gravitated toward Rich rosés in the winter. Now that I live in Los Angeles, where the temperature rarely falls below 65 degrees, I grab Crisp or Fruity wines pretty much all the time.

WHAT IF I LIKE IT ALL?

If you love all wines and really don't have a strong prevailing preference, the quiz and wheel won't identify your personal style category, but they can help you choose wines to fit your mood or for a specific time or occasion.

Enjoy yourself and have fun with it!

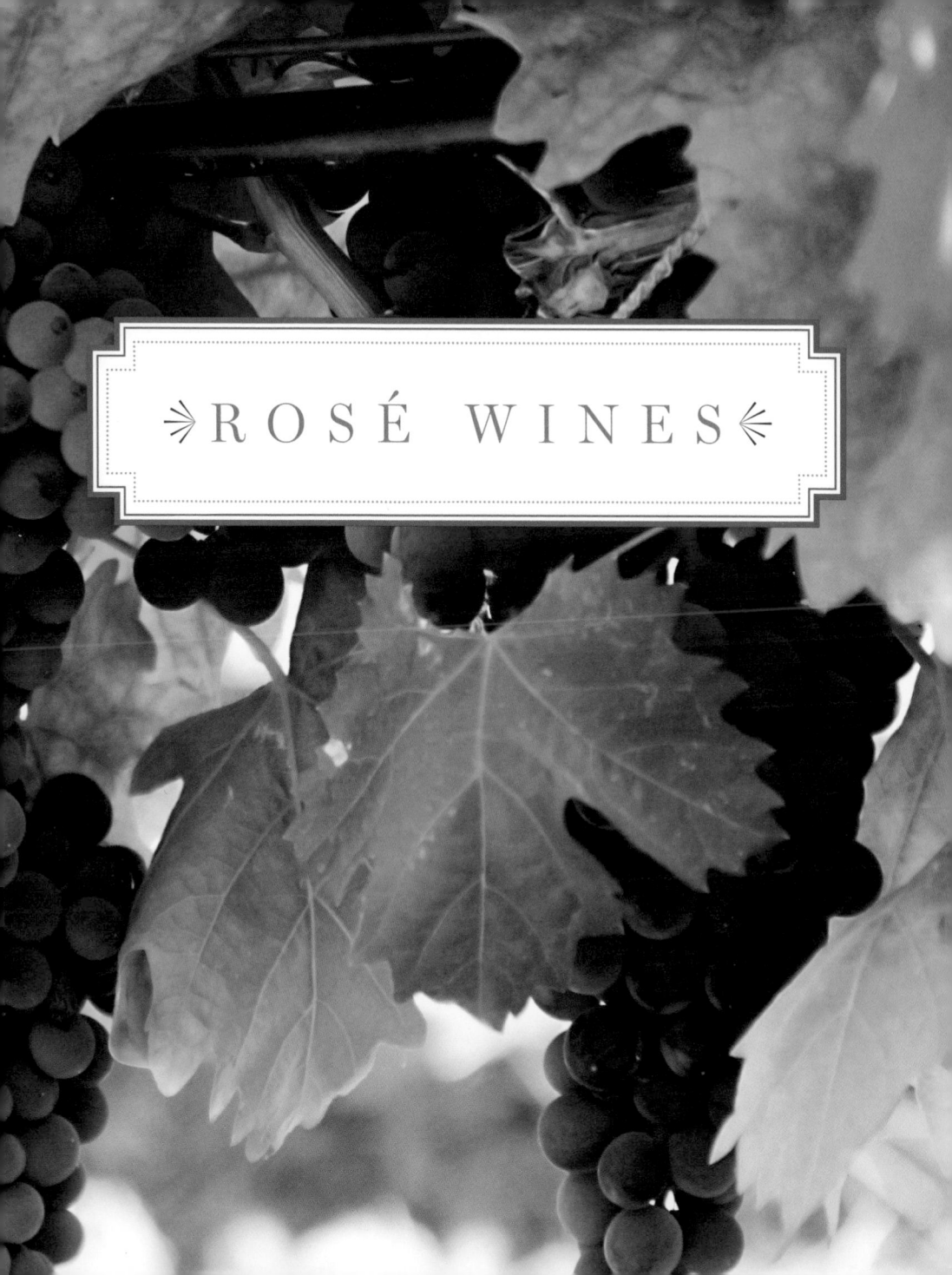

⇥ROSÉ WINES⇤

4

≫ BLUSH ≪

ILL CREEK WINERY—FOUNDED IN 1974 IN Sonoma Valley, California—purportedly coined the phrase "blush wine," but the sweet pink wine style has existed for ages. The internationally recognized category denotes a pink color, distinct fruitiness, and conspicuous sweetness.

If you fall into this category:

* You take your coffee or tea light and sweet—if at all.
* You enjoy white or milk chocolate over dark chocolate.
* You prefer sweet snacks to something salty or rich.
* You gravitate toward lighter, sweeter perfumes or colognes.
* You don't go for pure booze; no vodka, whiskey, or tequila straight up for you.

BLUSH CHARACTERISTICS

* True pink color
* Sweet: from delicate to dramatic. The human tongue generally can perceive sweetness in a liquid if it contains more than 5 grams of sugar per liter. (Many sodas contain more than 100 grams per liter.)
* Modest alcohol: 12 percent or lower.

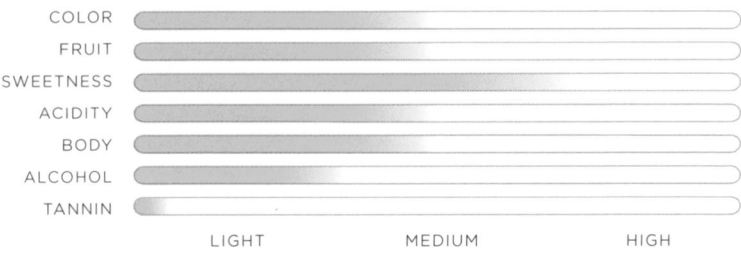

Blush wines are easy to drink and not so high in alcohol that they knock you over after the first or second glass. In other words, they're very user-friendly, so it's a shame that wine snobs have convinced people that dry is better and sweet is somehow less than. It's particularly ironic because people who prefer sweetness but abhor spicy food often can be what the hospitality industry calls super tasters (more taste buds than the average person). Some blush wines lack the quality indicators of balance, length, and complexity, true, but some of the best, longest-lived, and most expensive wines in the world are sweet: Madeira, Port, Riesling, Sauternes, and Tokaji—to name just a few. If sweet wine appeals to you, take pride in what you like, and don't let anyone blush-shame you!

Rosé Wine

WHITE ZINFANDEL

The Zinfandel grape grows only in red. In 1972, winemaker Bob Trinchero intensified one of Sutter Home Winery's Zinfandels by drawing off some of the free-run juice, which, following the French style, he then fermented and barrel-aged. He called it Oeil de Perdrix (Eye of the Partridge), a poetic term in France for white wines made from red grapes, but American laws require an English-language description, so the winery included "a white zinfandel wine" on the label. Three years later, Trinchero found himself with a "stuck" fermentation of another Zinfandel. When fermentation stopped prematurely, he had a sweet, pink, low-alcohol wine, which he marketed as White Zinfandel. He may not have been the first California winemaker to make pink wine from Zinfandel grapes, but he pushed it as a new style. Sales of Sutter Home White Zin soared from 25,000 cases in 1980 to more than 1.5 million in 1986.

Sutter Home White Zinfandel Napa Valley, California, USA

Today Sutter Home precisely controls the fermentation process. When the must reaches the desired level of color, alcohol, and sugar, they chill it, filter the yeast, and bottle it.

TASTING NOTES: Pale pretty pink with hard strawberry candy flavors, soft body, medium sweetness, and moderately low alcohol.

FOOD PAIRING: Spicy takeout. The sweetness of the wine will cool the jets of Kung Pao chicken, Szechuan shrimp, Thai curry, or the like, while enhancing the food's flavors.

PRICE: $6

WHITE MERLOT

Merlot is the most popular and most planted red grape in Bordeaux; it's also one of the most planted red grapes in California. Why? It's juicy and soft and has dark, black plummy flavors with lower bitterness than Cabernet Sauvignon and lower acidity than Pinot Noir. Those dark fruit notes carry into the blush and dry rosés made from it. When made in a dry style, the wine usually won't carry the designation "White Merlot," though. Instead, the winery usually calls it rosé of Merlot or just rosé without giving the grape variety. When you see "White Merlot," expect a blush style with some sweetness and moderately low alcohol.

Gallo Family White Merlot

Sonoma County, California, USA

In 1933, after Prohibition ended, brothers Ernest and Julio Gallo founded their eponymous winery in Modesto, California. Sixty years later it became America's largest winery, controlling a quarter of market share, and they still produce award-wining wines today.

TASTING NOTES: Pale bluish pink color with flavors of candied plum and a hint of tea leaves. On the palate, it has medium body, modest sweetness, and moderately low alcohol.

FOOD PAIRING: Spicy sushi. The sweetness of the wine will soften the spiciness of the wasabi, and the protein of the tuna or salmon will boost the plummy fruit flavors of the wine.

PRICE: $4

RED BLEND BLUSH

Many blush wines consist of a blend of red grape varieties, but the labels don't always say "blush" on them. An easy trick that you can use is looking at the alcohol by volume: if it's lower than 12 percent, chances are it has a little sweetness. The trick doesn't always work, particularly with New World wines, but try it the next time you want to drink something new.

Roscato Rosé Dolce Pavia, Lombardy, Italy

Made from Pinot Noir, Croatina, and Teroldego grapes, the must macerates with the skins at a low temperature before fermentation. When the wine reaches 8% ABV, the winemaker halts fermentation by dropping the temperature and then filtering the wine, leaving a residual sugar level of 90 grams per liter. In other words, it's a sweet one!

TASTING NOTES: Pale rose pink with tiny bubbles when poured. It smells like sweet strawberries and light cherry candy with a lusciously sweet palate of strawberry and a creamy finish.

FOOD PAIRING: Spicy dishes, such as a vindaloo, or desserts like lemon cake. Lemon and strawberry flavors complement each other nicely, and the dessert's acidity will enhance the fruit flavor of the wine.

PRICE: $14

MATEUS

The name of this blush wine comes from Mateus Palace, just north of the Douro Valley—birthplace of Port—in Portugal. Winemakers use ten different red and white grape varieties intended solely for this blush. Competing with Lancers, another famous postwar Portuguese wine, Mateus rose to fame in the 1970s, just before the ascent of White Zinfandel. The bottle has an iconic shape, like a bulbous flattened flask, similar to a German bocksbeutel. The popularity of Mateus has declined in America over the last few decades, but a revival is brewing, and Sogrape Vinhos, which owns the brand, makes a number of blush wines.

Sogrape Mateus "The Original" Porto, Portugal
Production grapes include Baga, Rufete, Tinta Barroca, and Touriga Franca, all red grapes indigenous to Portugal. Vinification follows the traditional method for white wines, and fermentation takes place slowly, with no skin contact, in temperature-controlled, stainless-steel vats before fining, cold-stabilization, filtering, and bottling.
TASTING NOTES: Very pale salmon color with a slight fizziness. Aromas include light red berries, floral notes, and a faint sea breeze. It has light body and off-dry sweetness (15 grams of residual sugar per liter) with moderate alcohol (11% ABV). The light prickle of bubbles raises the acidity slightly, making it more refreshing.
FOOD PAIRING: Appetizers, hors d'oeuvres, and tapas from sushi and ceviche to pork dim sum and beef kabobs.
PRICE: $6

THE FOUR MOST IMPORTANT
WINES IN THE WORLD

In 1966 I turned fourteen and landed my first job at a restaurant. Before the year was up, I had worked my way up from dishwasher to busboy and finally to waiter. I was as dumb as a box of rocks and knew nothing about wine. In fact, the restaurant served only beer and cocktails until this salesman from something called a 'distributor' asked to make a presentation to the floor staff. I was excited and even more so when he arrived and announced: 'Today, I have brought the four most important wines in the world, and I am going to give each of you the opportunity to taste them!' He carefully pulled out a bottle of Blue Nun, Lancer's Vinho Verde, Mateus Rosé, and Lancers Rosé. They were terrific, easy to drink, and easy to sell. With wine to sell and empowered with the newly acquired knowledge that 50 percent of the world's top wines were rosé, my check average and—most importantly—my tips increased dramatically.

"When I look back at the claim that this distributor representative had made concerning the importance of these wines, I realize that he was telling the truth. Lancers Rosé and Mateus Rosé introduced many to the world of wine and sold millions and millions cases in the United States and across the world."

—D. C. Flynt, MACH FLYNT/DC Flynt MW Selections

FUN FACT

At its peak in 1978, Mateus accounted for more than 40 percent of Portugal's total table wine exports. Worldwide sales reached 3.5 million cases that year.

VINHO VERDE ROSADO

Portugal's largest region, Vinho Verde lies north of Porto, near the border with the Galicia region in Spain. The name means "green wine," which accurately describes the lush countryside and its many terraced slopes. The most common wine made here is white, but the rosé comes from indigenous red varieties.

Broadbent Vinho Verde Rosé Vinho Verde, Portugal

This wine comes, in decreasing percentages, from Borraçal, Espadeiro, Amaral, and Vinhão grapes. According to the winery, "The trademark fizz of Vinho Verde wines derives from the release of carbon dioxide during malolactic fermentation," a secondary fermentation that takes place after the main alcohol fermentation.

TASTING NOTES: Medium fuchsia pink with slight effervescence. It has a light, crisp body, a scent of sea air, and 10% ABV. It tastes slightly sweet and very fruity, with notes of strawberry, cranberry, cherry, and minerals in the finish. The fizziness adds to the lightness and crispness of the wine, which otherwise would fall into the Crisp category—if not for the sweetness (14 grams of sugar per liter). An extremely well-balanced wine.

FOOD PAIRING: Traditional salted cod, which the Portuguese call bacalhau. Try it whipped with garlic and potatoes as a spread for small pieces of toasted baguette.

PRICE: $10

PINK MOSCATO

Muscat or Moscato is one of the oldest and most aromatic grape varieties in the world, but an ancient pedigree and full bouquet don't automatically equal popularity. Until recently, this variety was declining in both California and Italy.

The grape has many variations and clones—almost 200!—and comes in all colors: black, red, pink, white. Interestingly, all the variations and clones, regardless of color, share a distinct flavor not found in other grapes. That unique, easily identifiable taste likely explains why it has lasted so long and in so many different countries. Some people call it "grapey," which doesn't help. Others describe it as "soapy" or "kind of musky," which sounds like a perfume or cologne, so that doesn't help much either. My advice? Taste it and you'll remember it.

Pink Moscato comes from Muscat Blanc (white) grapes. To achieve the pink color and gain additional fruit flavors, vintners add red wine to the mix, but you won't find any of this information on the label or the producers' websites. For them, enjoying the wine is more about fun and approachability than imparting specific winemaking knowledge.

Pink Moscato is almost always low in acid and alcohol, which makes it a great wine for spicy foods. The sweetness can vary, though. Some producers provide a helpful sweetness scale on the label, but most don't. Nevertheless, Pink Moscato is a crowd-friendly wine. At any party, at least one or two people will enjoy it, and most bottles retail for less than $10 or $15, making it a good value.

Barefoot Bubbly Pink Moscato Sparkling Champagne

California, USA

Davis Bynum, a home winemaker, started Barefoot in 1965 and sold it some twenty years later to Michael Houlihan. Together, they focused on creating wines that were "not fussy" but also "affordable" and "quaffable" by listening to consumers rather than critics or connoisseurs. According to *Wines & Vines* magazine, Barefoot is America's bestselling brand today.

TASTING NOTES: Pale pretty pink in color with traditional flavors of sweet red fruit and hints of Mandarin orange, cherry, raspberry, and pomegranate. It has low acidity, low alcohol (9.5% ABV), a lot of fruit, and moderate sweetness.

FOOD PAIRING: Spicy barbecue. Pink Moscato can handle both the heat and sweetness of many barbecue sauces. The weight of this wine can stand up to anything from barbecue chicken to burgers. It's also good with chili dogs!

PRICE: $5

BRACHETTO

Wines made from the Brachetto grape—particularly in the northwestern Italian towns of Asti, Roero, and Alessandria—sparkle, taste sweet, and generally fall below 6 percent alcohol.

Rosa Regale Banfi Brachetto d'Aqui Spumante Piedmont, Italy
After the harvest, the Brachetto must macerates on its skins for two to three days, and winemakers use the Charmat Method—a second fermentation in stainless-steel tanks to create carbonation—prior to bottling.

TASTING NOTES: Deep red pink with strong flavors of strawberry, raspberry, and a hint of rose petal. It has full body, a prickle of bubbles, notable sweetness, soft acidity, and light alcohol.

FOOD PAIRING: Strawberry shortcake or strong, aromatic Italian cheeses, such as Taleggio.

PRICE: $20

FUN FACT

According to legend, Julius Caesar and Marc Antony presented Cleopatra with several containers of an early version of Brachetto d'Acqui, which she believed held the power to unleash the passions of her lovers. Find out for yourself next Valentine's Day!

Elio Perrone Bigarò Frizzante Piedmont, Italy

This wine is made from both Brachetto and Moscato grapes and also uses the Charmat Method for the second fermentation.

TASTING NOTES: Medium pink and bursting with floral, raspberry, and honey aromas. It tastes sweet and has low alcohol, medium body, and low acid offset with gentle effervescence.

FOOD PAIRING: Spicy barbecue or takeout followed by strawberry shortcake. The strawberries will complement the red berry flavors in the wine, and both the cake and the wine will taste better.

PRICE: $18

OFF-DRY SPARKLING ROSÉ

For sparkling wines, this is the sweetness scale from driest to sweetest: Brut Nature, Extra Brut, Brut, Extra Dry, Sec (dry), Demi-sec (semisweet), Doux (sweet). It's confusing, I know. When carbon dioxide dissolves in water, it forms carbonic acid, which adds extra acidity to the wine. To compensate and restore balance, winemakers increase the level of residual sugar in fully sparkling wines to around 15 grams per liter, which you definitely can perceive.

Prosecco comes from Glera, a white grape, and generally is made *frizzante* or slightly sparkling. It can have some sweetness to it, but, unlike with Pinot Grigio, winemakers can't soak the juice or wine on its skins to obtain a pink color. Instead, they must add red or pink grapes, juice, or wine. Italy is producing a good number of semisweet frizzante and *spumante* (fully sparkling) rosés made with white grapes and a little red wine added for color.

Cantine Riondo Pink Spago Argento Veneto, Italy

Glera, the grape that makes Prosecco, is a white variety, so to make it pink winemakers add a bit of red wine or coferment it with red grapes to achieve the desired pink hue. Then they use the Charmat Method to create the bubbles and, just before bottling, add the sugar, or *dosage*, to make it semisweet.

TASTING NOTES: Pale rose-petal pink with soft bubbles and light aromas of strawberry, white flowers, and minerals. It's semisweet, fairly light-bodied, and contains modest alcohol (10.5% ABV).

FOOD PAIRING: Spicy crab cakes. The semisweetness of the wine and its berry notes complement the sweetness of the crab, and the mild alcohol and acidity soften and harmonize with the spice.

PRICE: $11

Hello Kitty Sparkling Rosé Italy

Japan's Sanrio company created Hello Kitty in 1974, and more recently they teamed up with an Italian winemaker to create a Hello Kitty sparkling wine portfolio, which includes a sweet pink version. The wine uses a soft pressing of Pinot Noir grapes, followed by twenty-four hours of pulp-skin contact, and the Charmat Method.

TASTING NOTES: Pale peach color with floral, almond, and peach flavors. On the palate, it tastes semisweet with medium body and moderate alcohol.

FOOD PAIRING: Antonello Ristorante in Los Angeles pairs this wine with a special salad featuring microgreens, watermelon pieces shaped like Hello Kitty, feta cheese, and honey. They also recommend their pink bowtie pasta with a four-cheese alfredo sauce.

PRICE: $26

BERRY FRUIT ROSÉ WINE

Have you ever noticed, particularly on red or black grapes, a waxy white film that doesn't wash off? Naturally occuring yeast lives on the skins and forms what's called a grape's bloom. Grapes also have a good balance between sugar and acid that prevents yeast cells from dying too early in the fermentation process. If that happened, other microbes could digest those sugars and potentially create nasty acids and tastes. This happy equilibrium explains why people have been turning grapes into wine for thousands of years, but some wineries add berry fruit extract, such as strawberries, to grape wine to enhance the natural fruit flavors.

Pindar Summer Blush Long Island, New York, USA

This wine comes from a native Long Island grape called Suffolk, which belongs to the *Vitis labrusca* species, plus some natural strawberry flavor.

TASTING NOTES: Pale salmon color with intense tastes of white grape juice, candied strawberry, and tropical fruit, such as pineapple. It has medium to full body, medium sweetness, and soft texture with low acid and moderate alcohol (11.5% ABV). Strawberry and grape flavors linger in the long finish.

FOOD PAIRING: Try Jamaican chicken or a spicy curry over rice. The intense fruitiness of the wine goes toe to toe with the intense richness and spiciness of the dish. If you serve plantains with the Jamaican chicken—and you should—they will complement the tropical fruit notes in the wine.

PRICE: $11

André Strawberry Moscato Sparkling California, USA

Since 1966, André has striven to create easygoing wines that don't break the bank. They view every day as a celebration, so add some of their bubbles to your next brunch.

TASTING NOTES: Medium salmon pink color with flavors of juicy strawberry, watermelon, pomegranate, and peach. It has medium body, low alcohol (6.5% ABV), fruity sweetness, and a nice fizziness that adds some acidity.

FOOD PAIRING: Chips and spicy salsa. The acidity of the tomatoes in the salsa will balance the sweetness in the wine.

PRICE: $6

FUN FACT

As with red grapes, strawberries contain a compound called anthocyanin, which, like resveratrol—found in red grapes, such as Pinot Noir—has proven health benefits. The University of California at Los Angeles showed that anthocyanin-rich strawberry extract destroyed a particular kind of cancer cell more effectively than blueberry, cranberry, or blackberry extracts.

PINK SANGRÍA

An Iberian punch, sangría dates back at least to the eighteenth century, and the name derives from the Spanish word *sangre,* meaning blood, which describes the wine's color. Spanish restaurants first introduced it to America in the 1940s, and it sprang to national popularity here at the 1964 World's Fair. It has become a mainstay of summer brunches, although the EU ruled in 2014 that the name legally can apply only to products from Spain and Portugal. Red sangría is the most popular in terms of sales, but rosé sangrias are growing in stature, given their fun, summery color.

LVP Pink Sangria Spain

LVP stands for Lisa Vanderpump, a British-American actress, restaurateur, and TV personality best known for appearing on *The Real Housewives of Beverly Hills.* She and her daughter, Pandora, created this sangría from Garnacha and Bobal grapes.

TASTING NOTES: Deep rose petal pink with intense aromas of red berries, grapefruit, and orange. It smells like traditional sangría and tastes sweet, like intense candied red fruit, and as though it macerated with citrus fruit. It has medium body, soft acidity, and moderately low alcohol (10.5% ABV).

FOOD PAIRING: Spicy Mexican food. The sweetness and low acidity perfectly complement jalapeño heat. Also consider spicy chicken sandwiches or Buffalo wings; the tomatoes and meat in either of these dishes will augment the wine's cherrylike flavor.

PRICE: $12

FRUIT WINE

Other fruits, including strawberries, cherries, and cranberries, don't have the naturally occuring yeast bloom that grapes have, so if wine-makers use them they need to supply more sugar and grape yeast in the fermentation process to make berry fruit wine, also called country wine. Strawberries make a delicious blush wine that often tastes quite sweet, but here are a couple of alternatives for when you want to try something equally delicious but different.

The California Fruit Wine Co. Cranberry Wine
California, USA

Started by brothers Alan and Brian Haghighi in 2009, the California Fruit Wine Company creates wines with a social mission and long-term sustainability in mind. Look for this wine the next time you go to Whole Foods. TASTING NOTES: Deep red pink with intense aromas of candied cranberry and strawberry. It tastes very sweet, with notes of candied apple and strawberry jam, and features low alcohol. The cranberries give this wine a lot of acid, which cuts through the sweetness, leaving your palate refreshed—unlike many fruit wines that can taste like sucking on a lollipop.

FOOD PAIRING: Creamy, rich cheeses, such as Époisses, or blue cheeses, such as Roquefort and Stilton. Also try it with a rich New York–style cheesecake.
PRICE: $15

Gekkeikan Plum Wine Kyoto, Japan
Plum wine is enormously popular across Asia, but in America we see it most often in sushi restaurants. Producers can make it by soaking plums in distilled alcohol, by fermenting plum juice alone, or by adding plum flavor to grape or

rice wine (saké). This wine, made exclusively from fermented Ume plums from Wakayama Prefecture, Japan, ages for three years before release.

TASTING NOTES: Faint purplish pink color with intense aromas of candied plum and hints of apple and pear. It tastes very sweet and has low acidity, slightly warm alcohol (13% ABV), and full body.

FOOD PAIRING: Spicy sushi. The sweetness and low acidity of the wine will calm the spice, while the delicate plum flavor will contrast beautifully with any fish in the sushi, particularly tuna.

PRICE: $11

5

⇒ CRISP ⇐

If you fall into this category:

* You always put lemon on your fish, chicken, or green beans for extra kick.
* If you drink coffee or tea, you like it light and sweet.
* You enjoy white or milk chocolate over dark chocolate.
* You prefer juices with bite, such as lemonade or cranberry juice.
* You likely gravitate toward minty gum and salty or savory snacks.

CRISP CHARACTERISTICS

* Very pale to pale color
* Dry
* Light-bodied
* Low to minimal fruit
* Medium to high acidity

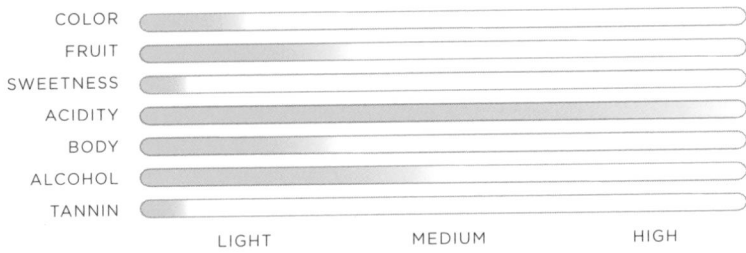

Most crisp rosé wines come from thin-skinned red grapes, or use the direct press or light maceration winemaking method, and some wines make use of all of the above. Others come only from pink grapes or white grapes with a little added red.

DIRECT PRESS ROSÉ

The direct press method applies white wine–making techniques to red grapes, maximizing delicate red berry flavors and often creating the lightest and driest rosés. Sometimes a winery also will use cold maceration, but duration makes a big difference. A short maceration on the skins can impart pale color, while long macerations, sometimes a few days, can yield fruitier or richer rosés.

Saint Aix AIX Rosé Côteaux d'Aix-en-Provence, France Maison Saint Aix began life in 1880 as a truffle orchard but became a vineyard in the early 1900s. They remain one of the largest domains in the Côteaux d'Aix-en-Provence appellation, and AIX is their top rosé blend, made with Grenache, Cinsaut, Syrah, and Counoise grapes and the direct press method.

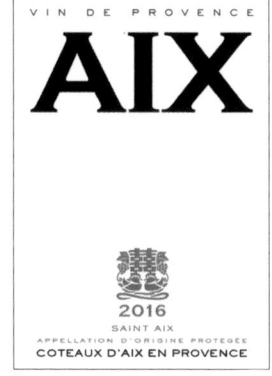

TASTING NOTES: Very pale, barely pink with moderately intense aromas of melon, citrus fruit, a whisper of strawberry, and a hint of sea air, minerality, and thyme in the finish. It tastes delicate and light, almost angular, with fresh bracing acidity and moderate alcohol (13% ABV) that can prove deliciously dangerous given its airiness.

FOOD PAIRING: Seafood and particularly fresh oysters, which enhance the minerality in the wine while also drawing out its savoriness.

PRICE: $18

PROVENCE ROSÉ

This region has been producing wine since the ancient Greeks colonized the area around 600 BC and brought wine with them. That long history makes Provence one of France's oldest winegrowing regions in addition to being the world's largest region specializing in rosé.

The vineyards here stretch for about 150 miles, and three appellations, or geographical indications, produce about 95 percent of Provençal rosé: Côtes de Provence, Côteaux d'Aix-en-Provence, and Côteaux Varois-en-Provence. Mainly Grenache, Cinsaut, Mourvèdre, and Syrah grow here, but up to 20 percent of the area has white grape varieties. It's illegal in Provence to make a rosé by blending white wine with red, but the law remains silent on pressing the grapes together.

Provence has a Mediterranean climate: rain mainly in fall and winter and enormous amounts of sunshine. A strong northwesterly wind, called the Mistral, crosses the region, reducing the risk of fungal disease and pestilence-bearing pests. As a result, it's easier to make organic wine here than elsewhere. If you're familiar with the spice blend herbes de Provence, you'll recognize the area's typical landscape: beautiful hillsides covered in wild lavender, rosemary, and thyme, which you can taste in the soft undertones of some of these rosés.

Clos Cibonne Tibouren Tradition Rosé Côtes de Provence, France
The estate's thirty-seven acres of vineyards lie just half a mile from the coast, surrounded by hillsides. This topography creates air circulation that allows for perfect maturation of the grapes and helps to reduce unwanted vintage variation. After harvest, the wines ferment in stainless-steel tanks and then age under fleurette (a thin veil of yeast) in century-old barrels.

TASTING NOTES: Delicate pale salmon color with modest aromatics of dried strawberry, baked bread, sea air, minerality, and blood orange. It tastes quite dry and refreshingly crisp with delicate body and 13.5% ABV. It has an elegance, a slight brininess, and yeastiness that recall Fino sherry and a hint of almond that suggests old oak maturation.

FOOD PAIRING: Pan bagnat, a popular Provençal sandwich filled with tuna, tomatoes, olives, and peppers, all steeped in an olive oil dressing.

PRICE: $26

FUN FACT

In 1797, the Roux Family purchased Clos Cibonne from Jean-Baptiste de Cibon, who had been captain of the royal marines under King Louis XVI.

Domaines Ott Mireille Clair de Noirs

Côtes de Provence, France

Clos Mireille has ancient terrain distinguished by its combination of schist and clay and an absence of limestone. Its proximity to the sea helps make for particularly fine wines. This wine costs more than most for Provence rosé, so what makes it so special? In a word: finesse. Harvesters pick the Grenache, Cinsaut, and Syrah grapes by hand, then strictly sort and select them. An extremely delicate pressing follows, with only short skin contact in the press, a slow fermentation, and between eight and twelve months' aging in vats.

TASTING NOTES: Very pale peach color with light aromas of fresh sea air, white peach, almond, a hint of lavender, and minerals in the finish. It tastes delicately light but has a roundness and balanced softness to the acidity that feels like falling into a pillow. It also has an incredible finish that lasts and lasts. Worth every dollar.

FOOD PAIRING: Simply prepared shellfish or fruits de mer, a plate of fresh seafood that can include shrimp, crab, mussels, and oysters with lemon wedges for squeezing to your acidity preference. The simple flavors augment the wine's complexity, and the wine's sea-breeze minerality complements the seafood. Also try brussel sprouts roasted in olive oil and garlic. The wine's softness calms the intensity of the sprouts' mustardy spiciness, and the two contrast beautifully together. Be careful, though: anything intensely flavored will overpower the wine.

PRICE: $50

AFFORDABLE ALTERNATIVES

Domaine La Rabiotte Rosé de Provence

Côteaux d'Aix-en-Provence, France

"The medium-bodied wine appears pale copper color and has pleasant aromas of berries and citrus with mineral tones. Higher acidity balances out in a surprisingly soft finish. It will cut through the fat of pulled pork without being overwhelmed. Sharp cheddar also pairs well with this wine."

PRICE: $13

Paul Ross, Seattle, USA

Domaine Fontaine du Clos Rosé

Provence, France

"This wine has a touch of salmon pink color with a light orange-red hue. Aromas include freshly crushed pomegranate with watermelon hints and a bouquet of strawberry jam. It starts with a charming, slightly dry watermelon taste and has beautiful, puckery acidity with a long finish."

PRICE: $11

—Monrick Croes, The Wine Room, Aruba

Herdade do Rocim "Mariana" Rosé Vidigueira, Alentejo, Portugal
This region features more rainfall and lower temperatures than its southern neighbors and has more of a reputation for its white wines than rosados. This wine is made from the free-run juice of Touriga Nacional and Aragonez grapes macerated for a very short time, cofermented with wild yeasts, fermented in a stainless-steel vat at 57°F for seventeen days, then bottle-aged for two months. This is a Provence-style wine at a more affordable price.

TASTING NOTES: Very pale flesh-tone with aromas of melon, elderflower, white peach, almond, and sea air.

FOOD PAIRING: Seafood brings out the wine's briny sea-air quality, and the wine will enhance the flavor of any fish you eat with it. Avoid tuna or salmon, however. Those powerfully flavored fishes will overpower this delicate wine.

PRICE: $11

FUN FACT

The name of this wine comes from the picturesque love story between Mariana Alcoforado, a nun at the Convent of Our Lady of the Conception in Beja, and Noël Bouton, Marquis de Chamilly, a French soldier stationed in Portugal. Her love letters to him were published and instantly became famous. He returned to his homeland, however, married, and eventually became marshal of France. History remembers her as Soror Mariana.

Wölffer Estate Rosé Long Island, New York, USA

As with White Zinfandel, many people assume White Merlot is a blush rosé, meaning it has conspicuous sweetness. However, if the label doesn't say "White Merlot" or "blush," if the primary grape is Merlot, and if the alcohol level exceeds 12 percent, then chances are it will taste dry. This blend contains almost half Merlot, a little more than a third Chardonnay, and then decreasing amounts of Cabernet Sauvignon, Cabernet Franc, Riesling, Pinot Noir, and Vignoles. Some of the blending takes place at the juice stage and some of it at the wine stage. Cool fermentation lasts up to eighteen days, and the wine gains extra depth from resting on its lees for six weeks.

TASTING NOTES: Very pale salmon pink color with aromas of pear, plum, and hints of peach. It tastes dry and light-bodied with ripe fruit, balanced acidity, and a lingering fruitiness on the palate. This elegant wine pairs well with many first-course dishes.

FOOD PAIRING: Hors d'oeuvres, such as soft goat cheese and tuna tartare.

PRICE: $18

Conundrum Rosé California, USA

This wine is made exclusively with Valdiguié grapes rolled for three hours before direct pressing, and it has a residual sugar level of just 1.4 grams per liter, making it a dry, crisp rosé.

TASTING NOTES: Medium peach color with sweet fruit aromas and a hint of lavender and strawberry. It tastes dry and has a candied strawberry fruitiness, medium weight, and a warming finish.

FOOD PAIRING: California or tuna rolls or tuna sashimi. The seafood's sweetness complements the wine's fruitiness and vice versa.

PRICE: $25

Michel Chapoutier Tournon Mathilda Rosé Victoria, Australia

Whole bunches of Grenache grapes are direct-pressed to obtain high-quality juice at low pressure and to reduce the extraction of color. The juice cold-settles without enzymes, and fermentation takes place at a low temperature with natural yeasts.

TASTING NOTES: Faint pink with soft aromas of sour cherry, lemon, and a hint of almond and matchstick. It tastes quite dry with light body, refreshing acidity, and 12% ABV.

FOOD PAIRING: Barbecued shrimp. The sweetness of the shrimp augments the fruitiness of the wine, while the grilling technique complements some of the wine's toasty qualities. Easy on the spice, though; otherwise you'll cover the light flavor of this wine.

PRICE: $14

PINOT NOIR ROSÉ

The Sancerre region lies at the eastern end of France's Loire Valley and has earned a reputation for producing world-class Sauvignon Blancs. If you like those white wines, chances are you'll like the rosés that come from here as well. The bracing acidity, light body, and generally pale color of Sancerre rosés come from Pinot Noir grapes, rather than Cabernet Franc, which dominates other areas of the Loire.

Pascal et Nicolas Reverdy Sancerre Terre de Maimbray Rosé

Sancerre, Loire Valley, France

Pinot Noir plats ferment at low temperatures with indigenous yeast in a combination of stainless-steel tanks and oak barrels.
TASTING NOTES: Pale pink with intense aromas of ripe strawberry, rose water, slight apricot, spice, and with oyster shells in the finish. It tastes crisply refreshing and, despite light body, has a roundness that will convince you that it's softer than it is. The flavor is a little fuller than the Côtes de Provence, but it has equal acidity.
FOOD PAIRING: Fried fish and in particular fish and chips. The acidity of the wine cuts through the fried batter, and even dressed with malt vinegar it will make the red fruit flavors come out more.
PRICE: $23

Smith Story Rosé of Pinot Noir Rheingau, Germany

Yes, Germany makes good Pinot Noir rosé, although here they generally call it Spätburgunder rosé. This example comes from Pinot Noir grapes pressed as whole clusters and tank-fermented.

TASTING NOTES: Very pale salmon pink with modest aromas of honeysuckle, strawberry, graphite minerality, and a hint of pear. It tastes lighter than air and has a bracing, cleansing acidity.

FOOD PAIRING: Light shellfish and dishes with delicate flavors, such as shrimp or oysters.

PRICE: $20

Carmel Road Barrymore Rosé of Pinot Noir

Monterey County, California

This celebrity wine is made in collaboration with Drew Barrymore, who, according to Lettie Teague of *The New York Times*, sends pictures of wines she likes to her winemaker and participates in the tasting process. She enjoys dry wines, or as she put it: "I will not dive into sweet waters."

TASTING NOTES: Pale pretty pink with aromas of ripe strawberry, pear, and white peach. On the palate, it tastes dry and light-bodied with balanced acidity and moderate alcohol.

FOOD PAIRING: Pinot Noir rosés have the most versatility in food pairings. This will pair with anything except perhaps a heavy New York strip steak.

PRICE: $17

GAMAY ROSÉ

As we saw in the chapter on making rosé, Beaujolais wine consists entirely of the Gamay grape variety. It's light and tastes of raspberry with barely any bitterness. In the Côtes de Toul region within Lorraine, it ranks as the most common grape variety for *vin gris*. Lorraine borders Germany, Belgium, and Luxembourg in the north, so it's no surprise that Côtes de Toul Gamay has much higher acidity than in Beaujolais and is deliciously delicate.

Lelièvre de Vin Gris de Toul

Côtes de Toul, Lorraine, France

This wine consists of 90 percent direct-pressed Gamay and Pinot Noir with 10 percent Auxerrois Blanc. Harvested by hand, the grapes tank-ferment, after which the wine ages for six months, four on fine lees.

TASTING NOTES: Pale orange-pink with soft aromas of fresh, sweet soft fruit: ripe blood orange, lime, and cranberry as well as honeysuckle and minerals. This lovely wine has light body, soft acid, and moderate alcohol, which makes it go down easy. It also has a fairly long finish, unusual for rosés at this price.

FOOD PAIRING: Turkey tetrazzini, which has a buttercream and parmesan sauce made with white wine or sherry. Keep it in mind for Thanksgiving as well!

PRICE: $15

LOIRE RED BLEND ROSÉ

The Loire Valley produces incredible Sauvignon Blancs—Sancerre and Pouilly-Fumé for example—as well as Chenin Blancs, but great red grapes also grow here: Cabernet Franc, specifically from Chinon, and Pinot Noir, which makes superb Sancerre rosés. Today winemakers are blending these two varieties and others, such as Gamay and Négrette.

J. Mourat Collection Rosé

Fiefs Vendéens Mareuil, Loire Valley, France

A pneumatic press gently presses Pinot Noir, Cabernet Franc, Négrette, and Gamay Noir grapes, which then cold-settle in steel tanks.

TASTING NOTES: Pale salmon pink with modest aromas of strawberry, grapefruit, citrus, faint herbs, and wet stone. This refreshing crowd-pleaser tastes dry and light-bodied with crisp acidity and moderate alcohol.

FOOD PAIRING: Seafood, particularly shrimp and crab bisque, and quiche Lorraine go particularly well with this wine. The ham's sweetness brings out the wine's fruitiness.

PRICE: $15

FUN FACT

According to legend, the Knights Templar introduced the Négrette grape from the Near East to France. As a red wine, it tends to taste floral and sometimes gamy or meaty.

AUSTRIAN ROSÉ

Zweigelt, a cross between the Blaufränkisch and St. Laurent varieties, is Austria's most planted and most popular red grape variety. It generally has high acidity though not as much as Pinot Noir. Blaufränkisch ranks second in popularity, and you'll find rosés made from it as well. Austria also produces some gently sparkling Pinot Noir rosés that taste even lighter and tarter than when made as still wines.

Some Austrian vintners make saignée rosés, but most often Zweigelt sees a few short hours of maceration, or skin contact, before pressing, which gives it its pale color.

Petra Unger "Q" Rosé, Kremstal, Austria

Harvesters pick the Zweigelt grapes two weeks before those for red Zweigelt. The fruit, which is less mature and has higher acid, is destemmed, crushed, and then given two hours of maceration for color before pressing. The rosé ferments slowly for a week at a low temperature in a steel tank, where it ages on its lees until the end of November before filtering and bottling in December.

TASTING NOTES: Very pale peach color with aromas of light cranberry, pear, a hint of white pepper, and minerals. It has light body, refreshingly crisp acidity, and more fruitiness on the palate than on the nose.

FOOD PAIRING: Wiener Schnitzel, which is veal or pork pounded thin, lightly breaded, and then fried. The high acidity of the wine cuts through the fat of the breading, and the berry aromas augment and contrast with the meat.

PRICE: $15

CHIARETTO

This dry style—which means "little light"—comes from near Lake Garda in Lombardy, Italy. The lake has a moderating effect, cooling the region and the grapes in the summer and warming them in the winter. Chiarettos use red grapes and white wine–making practices, similar to Provence. Winemakers often use Corvina, the primary grape in the famous Amarone wines, as well as other indigenous varieties.

Costaripa RosaMara Valtènesi Chiaretto Garda Classico

Lombardy, Italy

Winemakers use Groppello, Marzemino, Sangiovese, and Barbera grapes and the Lacrima Method, which uses static dripping, or stationary draining, before fermentation. (This "tear-drop" technique produces free-run juice, much like a gentle direct pressing.) Half of the must ferments and ages in small oak barrels for around six months, and the other half in stainless steel.

TASTING NOTES: Very pale peach color with aromas of sea air, flowers, almond, and hints of pomegranate. It has light body, round texture, and balanced, refreshing acidity.

FOOD PAIRING: Risotto in general and risotto alla Milanese, made with saffron, in particular.

PRICE: $21

PINOT GRIS ROSÉ

The Pinot Gris grape naturally has a pink tinge. Even when made into a white wine, it has a slightly pinkish hue. Winemakers can use a number of techniques to capture the grapes' color and make pink wine from a grape traditionally used to make white wine.

Raidis Estate Pinot Gris Rosé Cheeky Goat Coonawarra, Australia

In Australia, vintners make a number of rosés with Rhône Valley varieties (Grenache, Syrah, Mourvèdre). Raidis Estate took a chance, though, planted Pinot Gris, and it worked! They let the grapes hang longer on the vine than others, which allows the natural pink color to deepen as the grapes ripen. The pre-fermentation maceration of the wine lasts for four days, which also transfers more color from the skins to the wine.

TASTING NOTES: Very pale peach color with intense aromas of honeysuckle, orange blossom, light apricot, and peach. On the palate it's fairly light, perhaps more on the medium side, but the acidity is crisp and bright and has a fruitiness that belies a New World wine. The texture is round and fine and has a long finish.

FOOD PAIRING: The Fabulous Ladies' Wine Society recommends Tarte Flambée, a traditional Alsatian flatbread with bacon and cheese.

PRICE: $20

WHITE GRAPE RIOJA ROSADO

Rioja rosado can be made in a variety of ways. White grapes with a bit of red grapes to macerate or coferment, or a splash of red wine can create a light-bodied, Crisp-style rosé. Those made from only red grapes make Fruity-style rosés, while Spanish red grapes using the saignée method lean toward the Rich style. Some labels indicate the grape varieties but not whether they're white or black or how it's made. In which case, look at the color. If it appears very light, chances are it's made with predominantly white grapes with a little red to add some pink.

CVNE Viña Real Rosado Rioja, Spain

Viura (white, 85 percent) and Tempranillo (red, 15 percent) grapes comacerate for six hours before undergoing a gravity bleed (the Lacrima Method, page 103) to create the must. Fermentation takes place in stainless-steel tanks below 60°F for 20–25 days before cold maceration.

TASTING NOTES: Pale salmon pink with faint aromas of citrus, cranberry, white flowers, slices of fresh almonds, and minerals. It tastes dry and has moderate acidity and alcohol. This wine falls on the cusp between Crisp and Fruity, but it's not quite fruity enough for the Fruity category.

FOOD PAIRING: Dim sum—chicken, pork, prawns, or vegetables. Nothing too rich, which will overpower the wine.

PRICE: $14

TXAKOLIN GORRIA

The Txakolina style hails from the Basque region of northern Spain and has been made since at least 1520, when a document mentions *vino chacolín* (the Spanish spelling). It was generally a homemade wine until Spanish regulations recognized official regional designations for it in 1989. It's lightly sparkling, like Italian frizzante, with high acidity and low alcohol. The most popular version in America is white, but production of rosé versions (*gorria*) is increasing along with global demand for all things rosé.

Ameztoi Getariako Txakolina Rubentis Basque Region, Spain
This wine is made from the Hondarrabi Zuri (white, 50 percent) and Hondarrabi Beltza (red, 50 percent) varieties. Secondary fermentation takes place in the bottle, as with cava and champagne, and it ages on its lees for fourteen months— longer than cava but shorter than champagne.
TASTING NOTES: Very pale pink with soft aromas of lime, grapefruit, and light strawberry fruit with minerals. It finishes with some yeasty notes of baked bread. The slight prickle of bubbles makes it taste dry and crisp, though, and it has delicate body and moderately low alcohol (10.5% ABV).
FOOD PAIRING: Light hors d'oeuvres, such as oysters, sushi, or fish tempura.
PRICE: $25

BLANC DE NOIRS SPARKLING

Champagne is France's most northerly region to grow red grapes, which makes for a highly acidic, very crisp style of wine. The carbon dioxide also adds acidity and makes the body even lighter. By law, producers can make champagne from one or more of three grapes: Pinot Noir, Pinot Meunier, and Chardonnay. The first two are both red grapes, and Champagnes made from them are called blanc de noirs, which literally means "white from blacks." Winemakers direct-press the grapes for the base wine, which appears slightly pink before the second fermentation. This process creates a pale, crisp, delicate, highly complex rosé.

Egly-Ouriet Blanc de Noirs Grand Cru Les Crayères Vieilles Vignes

Ambonnay, Champagne, France

This champagne comes from a single Grand Cru vineyard in the Montagne de Reims region of Champagne. It contains 100 percent Pinot Noir grapes from 70-year-old vines. It ferments

and ages on its lees for more than five years in barrels (25 percent in new barrels).
TASTING NOTES: Very pale, barely there, fleshy pink with incredible complexities of citrus fruit, hint of strawberry, minerals, baked brioche, and buttered toast. It tastes very dry, crisp, and delicate, and the persistent small bubbles fully sparkle. It has a long finish and incredible finesse.
FOOD PAIRING: Chapon de fête au Champagne—roasted chicken in Champagne sauce served with sliced potatoes pan-fried in butter, duck fat, parsley, and garlic. These simple flavors bring out the wine's subtle berry notes and augment the notes of baked brioche in the wine.
PRICE: $160

René Jolly Blanc de Noirs Brut Champagne

Champagne, France

Made with 100 percent organically grown Pinot Noir, this traditional method sparkling wine ages for three years in the bottle on its lees.

TASTING NOTES: Pale yellow gold with a rose tint and intense aromas of citrus, white peach, and strawberry with mineral and biscuit notes. Very dry on the palate, it sparkles fully and has medium body with very crisp acidity, exceptional balance, and great length.

FOOD PAIRING: Fried chicken or french fries. Seriously! The acidity of the champagne cuts the oil, making the food taste lighter than it is. The wine's biscuity notes also complement the flavor of the meat or potatoes while the slight strawberry notes offer contrast, making all the flavors more prominent.

PRICE: $30

Schramsberg Blanc de Noirs Brut Vintage

North Coast, California, USA

About a third of this sparkling wine—made from Pinot Noir (88 percent) and Chardonnay (12 percent)—ferments in barrels before the secondary fermentation in bottles. The final wine has 11 grams of residual sugar per liter, so you might perceive just a hint of sweetness amid the invigorating acidity. TASTING NOTES: Pale yellow gold with slight pink hue and aromas of baked pastry, strawberry, and buttered toast. It tastes crisp and dry and has small, persistent bubbles, fine mousse, light body, and moderate alcohol (12.7% ABV). FOOD PAIRING: Soft and nutty cheeses or macadamia-crusted halibut, a light-bodied white fish that matches the weight of the wine. The acidity in the liquid cuts the nuts' richness, but its pastry notes nicely complement them. PRICE: $35

6

⇒ FRUITY ⇐

This category contains wines that, above anything else, taste obviously ripe, juicy, and fruity. If you fall into this style:

* You drink your coffee or tea with some milk and sugar but not a lot.
* You sometimes put lemon on your fish, chicken, or green beans but not always.
* You prefer orange or apple juice to cranberry juice or fruit punch.
* You like a little spice in your food but not too much.
* You chew fruity gum rather than mint or bubblegum.
* You enjoy eating fruit snacks more than candy, chocolate, or something salty.

FRUITY CHARACTERISTICS

* Overt fruit—the most prominent feature
* Medium body, whether medium light or medium high
* Stronger color and concentration
* Medium acidity, whether medium light or medium high

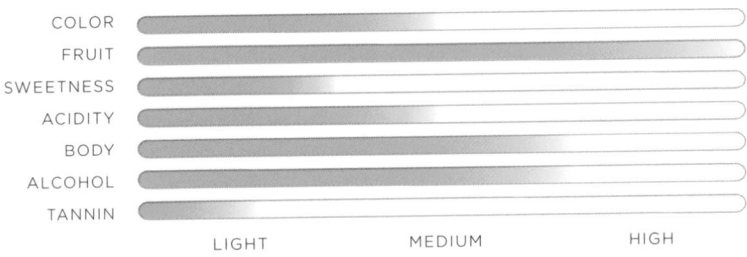

COLOR
FRUIT
SWEETNESS
ACIDITY
BODY
ALCOHOL
TANNIN

LIGHT   MEDIUM   HIGH

Many of these wines come from a moderate to warm climate. The more sunlight, the higher the temperature, and the better the drainage, the riper the grapes become, yielding fruitier wines. Save for the sparklers, all these wines come from red grapes. The juice for the still wines (no bubbles) that follow undergoes a few hours of maceration on the skins before fermenting—different from the direct press method we saw in the Crisp chapter. Winemakers often maintain cold temperatures before, during, and/or after fermentation, which helps the wine retain its fruitiness. You won't find any oak influence here, either, which doesn't maintain cold temperatures as well as steel tanks. Oak also allows for micro-oxygenation, which can reduce fruitiness over time. For the sparkling wines, rather than the direct press method as with blanc de noirs in the Crisp chapter, winemakers add a little fruity red wine to achieve the desired level of color and red berry fruitiness.

CABERNET FRANC ROSÉ

Cabernet Franc is one of the parents of Cabernet Sauvignon. It has relatively thick skin and gives rich raspberry flavors with less bitterness than its more popular offspring. In the Loire Valley, pretty much anywhere west of Sancerre, most producers make rosés from Cabernet Franc, and they generally use a pre-fermentation cold soak more than the direct press or saignée methods.

Domaine du Grand Breviande Chinon Rosé

Chinon, Loire Valley, France

Chinon lies within the region of Touraine and has earned a reputation for making high-quality red wine entirely from Cabernet Franc, like this rosé.

TASTING NOTES: Deep salmon pink with aromas of ripe, luscious raspberry fruit, herbes de Provence, spice, and minerals. It has medium-high body with rich, full fruit flavors. For a Loire rosé, it offers very good balance between acidity and alcohol.

FOOD PAIRING: Charcuterie, such as saucisson, terrines, pâtés, or confit. Also try mild cheeses, such as Monterey Jack, Gruyère, or white cheddar. Don't forget the baguette!

PRICE: $14

MEMORIES OF CHINON

"The most memorable rosé I've ever had was from the Loire Valley. I was on my honeymoon, and yet there is another reason that I will never forget that wine. The winery was small, tucked behind the hedges of green for which Chinon is known. The winemakers were a husband-and-wife couple, who moved about their winery in the way a comfortable, happy couple does. The husband poured me a taste, the eyes of his wife crinkling into a smile. Delicious! Of course, I wanted this wine for our picnic.

"He then presented to us a slender bottle of the Cabernet Franc wrapped in paper.

"A gift, but why? I thought.

"The winemaker's eyes watered, and as he spoke he took his wife's hand: 'You are American, and many years ago an American soldier saved my life and this farm. I will never forget it.'

"And I will never forget that winemaker or his rosé."

—Pam Dillon, cofounder and CEO, Wine Ring

BORDEAUX ROSÉ

At the 2012 London International Wine Fair, François Millo, president of the Provence Wine Council, said that "People who make saignée rosé are opportunists. In their mind, they are making red wine—the rosé just happens to be a by-product. The saignée method is a bad way of making rosé." Since then, rosé production has been increasing in Bordeaux, which seems to have heard Millo's disparagement as a call to action. Château Brown in Pessac-Léognan, for example, released its first rosé in 2013. "Rosé can be a serious wine, and Bordeaux can make serious rosé," said Jean-Christophe Mau of Château Brown to *Drinks* magazine. "We need to change people's perceptions."

Bordeaux rosés often contain blends of Merlot, Cabernet Sauvignon, Cabernet Franc, Petit Verdot, Carménère, and increasingly Malbec. Merlot accounts for two-thirds of plantings here and dominates Bordeaux blends, including rosés.

Château de Sours La Fleur d'Amelie Bordeaux Rosé Bordeaux, France
The juice from Merlot, Cabernet Franc, and Cabernet Sauvignon grapes soaks with the skins for several hours before a gentle pressing. Fermentation takes place in stainless-steel tanks over twenty-eight days at 57°F. Then the wine rests on its lees, with regular stirring to build depth and texture.
TASTING NOTES: Medium pink with intense aromas of cranberry, plum, tea leaf, and a refreshingly bright mineral note. It has medium body, soft acidity, and moderate alcohol.
FOOD PAIRING: Poisson à la Bordelaise, a local dish made with white fish, usually cod or hake, covered with a paste made of bread, shallots, garlic, lemon, white wine, salt and pepper before baking. The heartiness of the dish stands up nicely to the wine.
PRICE: $10

Domaine Clarence Dillon Clarendelle Rosé Bordeaux, France

This blend of Merlot, Cabernet Sauvignon, and Cabernet Franc undergoes pre-fermentation maceration before pressing, fermentation at low temperature, and aging on its lees.

TASTING NOTES: Pale pink with aromas of ripe red and black currant, cranberry, tea leaf, and minerality in the finish. On the palate, it's middle-of-the-road everything: weight, acidity, and alcohol, which makes a great crowd-pleaser.

FOOD PAIRING: Baked brie with cranberries and walnuts on top.

PRICE: $14

D'OC ROSÉ

On the Mediterranean coast, France's Languedoc region has warm, dry, sunny summers and wet winters. Winemakers here blend the same grapes that their Provençal counterparts use, but to make the wine they use maceration rather than direct press, which allows for more fruit in the finished wine.

Domaine de Sainte Rose Coquille d'Oc Servian, France

Growers hand-harvest the fruit of this GSM blend early in the ripening season. The juice ferments in stainless-steel tanks, and the wine ages for more than four months.

TASTING NOTES: Medium peach color with juicy ripe aromas of red cherry, light raspberry, pear, grapefruit, and minerals. It tastes dry and has medium body and soft acid, with slight warming alcohol in the finish.

FOOD PAIRING: Salad with grilled shrimp will enhance the wine's cherry taste, and the wine will enliven the flavors of the shrimp.

PRICE: $16

RED GRAPE SPANISH ROSADO

The International Organisation of Vine and Wine ranks Spain as the second biggest producer of rosé, with more than 145 million gallons in 2014, about 20 percent of worldwide production. Spanish rosados primarily sell on the export market, whereas the opposite holds true in France, where production doesn't fully meet domestic demand. Many Spanish rosados ride the line between the Crisp and Fruity styles, but here's a helpful rule: (1) rosados made with predominantly white grapes with a bit of red wine added for color or (2) those using red grapes but white wine-making methods tend to taste lighter and crisper than those made only with macerated red grapes. Rosados made with red grapes and pre-fermentation maceration lean more toward the Fruity style

La Granja 360 Garnacha Rosé

Cariñena, Aragon, Spain

Manually harvested Garnacha grapes go through destemming and pressing before fermenting in stainless-steel tanks at 79°F for twenty-five days. A ten-day maceration follows, then malolactic fermentation and the final microfiltration. Buy a bottle or two the next time you see it at Trader Joe's.
TASTING NOTES: Deep pink with rich flavors of cherry and black cherry and with notes of rose and minerals in the finish. It tastes dry but with concentrated fruit, and it also has some spice in the finish.
FOOD PAIRING: Elevate this great-value wine with some simple tapas: jamón Ibérico, pork belly medallions, or migas (fried bread and chorizo with eggs).
PRICE: $5

Bodegas Olivares Jumilla Rosado

Finca Hoya de Santa Ana, Jumilla, Murcia, Spain

This wine contains 70 percent Garnacha and 30 percent Monastrell grapes, which macerate on their skins.

TASTING NOTES: Pale salmon pink with fruity aromas of candied cherry and blackberry and with hints of flowers, spice, and minerals in the finish. It tastes dry and has medium body, modest acidity, and balanced alcohol.

FOOD PAIRING: Zarangollo, a Murcian dish like a cross between ratatouille and an omelet, made from tomatoes, eggplant, onions, and eggs. The acidity of the tomatoes complements the fruitiness of the wine, and the earthy protein from the egg balances everything. A great regional pairing for your next brunch!

PRICE: $10

FUN FACT

Unlike many European wine regions, Jumilla has an official wine route, the Ruta del Vino de Jumilla. Check out its wineries the next time you visit southeastern Spain.

El Coto Rioja Rosado Rioja, Spain

This traditional half-and-half blend of Tempranillo and Garnacha grapes comes from El Coto and other vineyards in the Rioja Alavesa sub-region. The wine macerates on the skins for 48 hours to extract flavor and color before cold fermentation and bottling.

TASTING NOTES: Gorgeous pink color with luscious aromas of ripe cherry, strawberry, and watermelon and a slight hint of spice and herbs. Rounded with soft acidity, this dry wine bursts with fruitiness and features a slightly warming finish.

FOOD PAIRING: Tapas or hors d'oeuvres, such as ham croquettes or fresh prawns in olive oil with garlic and chile peppers.

PRICE: $11

TUSCAN ROSATO

Sangiovese, the main grape that grows in Tuscany's warm climate, makes the famous wines of Chianti and Brunello di Montalcino. The grape has high acidity and in cool years can develop green tannic astringency, although increasingly warming temperatures mean that's happening less and less these days. Tuscan rosatos can run the price gamut from less than $10 to more than $50, so there's something here for every budget.

Il Poggione Brancato Rosato di Toscana Montalcino, Italy

After harvest, the Sangiovese must remains in contact with the skins for twenty-four hours followed by a long, cool fermentation.

TASTING NOTES: Medium pink with aromas of strawberry and cherry and hints of minerals and herbs. It has medium body and balanced acidity and alcohol, as well as a juicy fruit finish.

FOOD PAIRING: Octopus prepared with salt, garlic, and olive oil. The easy richness of the octopus—richer than other seafood, though not as rich as salmon or tuna—brings out the wine's flavors.

PRICE: $17

FUN FACT

The word Sangiovese derives from "*sanguis Jovis,*" or Jupiter's blood, the name that the monks of Santarcangelo di Romagna gave it centuries ago.

CERASUOLO

Cerasuolo means "cherry-red" in Italian. The Abruzzo region makes a rosato called Cerasuolo d'Abruzzo, which undergoes a short maceration on its skins before pressing.

Fantini Farnese Cerasuolo d'Abruzzo

Abruzzo, Italy

The harvest of the Montepulciano grapes takes place in early October. After destemming and pressing, maceration on the skins lasts about six hours to achieve the desired hue, followed by racking and fermentation without skins for fifteen days at around 54°F.

TASTING NOTES: Soft pink with modest aromas of boysenberry, sour cherry, and blood orange. It has a slight savory or herbal taste and minerality that point to the Old World winemaking style while still maintaining balanced acidity and fruitiness with slightly warm alcohol.

FOOD PAIRING: Charcuterie or antipasti. The savory protein of the meats and hard cheeses contrasts nicely with the fruitiness of the wine.

PRICE: $10

DRINKER BEWARE

Don't confuse Cerasuolo d'Abruzzo wine with Cerasuolo di Vittoria, an official winemaking region in Sicily. Ditto the Montepulciano grape, which grows chiefly in Abruzzo, with Montepulciano the town in Tuscany, which specializes in the Sangiovese grape.

SOUTHERN ITALIAN ROSATO

In southern Italy, the weather is warmer and sunshine more prevalent, which makes red grape varieties with thicker skins that in turn make for richer red wines. When made into rosatos, they taste fresh, lively, fruity, and dry.

Thirty years ago, the thought of Sicilian wine instantly called Marsala and fortified wines to mind. In the last decade, though, Sicilian wines have exploded onto the American market and are growing worldwide. Figures suggest a 30 percent increase in sales between 2014 and 2015 with no sign of slowing. Today many people know Nero d'Avola, a Sicilian red, but Nerello Mascalese—an indigenous cross between Sangiovese and Manonico Bianco from the slopes of Mount Etna—makes for many high-quality rosatos. The soils around Europe's highest active volcano are rich and fertile and have well-draining slopes, perfect for viticulture.

Cantele Negroamaro Rosato Salento, Puglia, Italy
The grapes macerate for 12–24 hours to extract color from the skins and obtain the classic aromatic notes of the Negroamaro grape. The free-run must ferments at around 58°F in stainless-steel vats.

TASTING NOTES: Medium pink with slight orange hues, this user-friendly wine has subtler though still fruity aromas of cherry, cranberry, and blood orange. It tastes dry and has medium body with moderate acidity and alcohol.

FOOD PAIRING: Cheese or vegetable omelets or eggs Benedict contrasts nicely with the fruity taste of this wine. In other words, drink it with brunch!

PRICE: $12

Girolamo Russo Etna Rosato Etna, Sicily, Italy

Growers pick the Nerello Mascalese grapes early in the season, and the winemaker presses the clusters whole before they macerate briefly with the skins. The wine matures in steel tanks.

TASTING NOTES: This wine appears pale salmon pink, but it bursts with aromas of strawberry, blood orange, cherry, and minerals. On the palate, it has medium-light body and tastes crisp and fruity—like a day at the beach!

FOOD PAIRING: Pasta with sardines and fennel, an ancient, seasonal Sicilian dish, harmonizes beautifully with this wine.

PRICE: $24

ISRAELI ROSÉ

Israel generally has a hot Mediterranean climate, so growers tend to plant grapes here at higher altitudes. Geographically this is an Old World region, but many winemakers follow more of a New World production style, which puts their wines firmly in the Fruity category. Many critics count the Judean Hills and Galilee as Israel's top winemaking regions. The Judean Hills area has great promise, given its location, relatively high altitude, and thin limestone soils, but it's still developing. Israel's wine production and per capita consumption are still both quite small. In 2011, the average Israeli drank less than one bottle per year, while the average American drank a bottle per month. That said, both production and quality here are rising.

Flam Rosé Judean Hills, Israel

Cabernet Franc grapes cold-macerate on their skins for several hours for color, then cold-ferment in stainless-steel tanks for three weeks to enhance the flowery aromas of fresh red fruit.
TASTING NOTES: Deep salmon color with very ripe, fruity aromas of raspberry with notes of violet, herbs, mint, minerals, and orange blossom. It tastes dry, has medium-full body and crisp acidity, and finishes clean and refreshing with a hint of bitters.
FOOD PAIRING: Johannes Marlena of The Corkscrewer Report recommends grilled salmon or lox, brisket, hot pastrami, or corned beef in a club sandwich or wrap. Grilled salmon highlights the wine's savory nature; lox brings out its refreshing lemon notes; while corned beef makes the raspberry notes pop.
PRICE: $30

FLAM ROSÉ
BONUS TASTING NOTE

"Elegant soft pink with a slight salmon hue. Medium viscosity. Bright, grassy notes with subtle stone fruit aromas—nectarines and white peaches. Ever so slightly sweet on the palate with noticeable minerality. Creamy mouthfeel, warming alcohol, but bone-dry! With pleasant acidity and a long finish, it ends on a note of the local pomelo fruit. Very well balanced. Perfect for celebrating a long weekend, brunch with friends, or any summer afternoon."
—Tim Tranchilla, U.S. Embassy, Tel Aviv

FUN FACT

Most of Israel's wines qualify as kosher, though not all. For those that do, restrictions begin as soon as the grapes enter the winery. The main difference between kosher and non-kosher wine is who touches it, and Sabbath-observant orthodox Jews must supervise the entire process for a wine to certify as kosher.

NEW WORLD RHÔNE BLEND ROSÉ

From the Rhône Valley down through Provence, southeastern France burns bright as a hotspot for rosé wines. Many of the grapes that grow here—Grenache, Syrah, Mourvèdre, Cinsaut—make for even more overtly fruity wines in the New World, particularly when made with a pre-fermentation soak, in stainless-steel tanks, and under cool fermentation temperatures. This process allows the wines to retain their bright color and zesty fruity flavor.

Badenhorst Family Wines Secateurs Rosé

Swartland, South Africa

Growers pick the Cinsaut and Grenache grapes early in the morning, and the bunches undergo pressing slowly so as not to extract too much color. Shiraz (Syrah) juice separately goes through two hours of skin contact before pressing. The winemaker blends the juices, which then ferment in steel tanks before rough filtration.

TASTING NOTES: Pale salmon pink with strong aromas of strawberry (Cinsaut) along with mineral notes. This fruity diamond in the rough tastes of raspberry (Shiraz) yet has light body and a flavorfully broad mid-palate (Grenache). It finishes clean with lovely finesse.

FOOD PAIRING: Poached salmon. The wine's acidity heightens the salmon's flavor without overwhelming it. The savory protein will push the wine's fruit forward even more.

PRICE: $15

Le P'tit Paysan Pierre's Pirouette Rosé of Mourvèdre San Benito County, California
Growers pick the Mourvèdre, Grenache, and Cinsaut grapes at just the right time to maintain a bright, natural acidity. Fermentation takes place in several lots with both native and cultured yeasts.
TASTING NOTES: Soft pink with fruity aromas of strawberry and cranberry and

then hints of boysenberry, herbaceousness, and stoniness in the finish. It tastes dry but is otherwise middle of the road across the board: body, acidity, and alcohol.
FOOD PAIRING: Salmon lox or cured salmon. The protein enhances the wine's red fruit tastes, while the wine's acidity sharpens the flavor of the salmon.
PRICE: $19

SPARKLING ROSÉ

Blanc de noirs champagnes fall on the cusp with white wines. With true sparkling rosés, winemakers use a much fruitier style. Vintage rosé champagnes—made exclusively from grapes of the same year, not old wine—stand as the exception to that general rule because they age on their lees for at least three years. The longer that champagne or champagne-style wine ages in the bottle, the less fruity and more toasty it becomes, meaning that it will taste more liked baked pastry with a hint of strawberries instead of strawberries with a hint of baked pastry.

Pata Negra Cava Rosé Brut Catalonia, Spain
Consisting of Trepat (80 percent), a red grape native to Catalonia, and Pinot Noir (20 percent), this wine is made using the Traditional Method. Secondary fermentation takes place in the bottle, and it ages for twelve months.
TASTING NOTES: Medium deep pink with rich aromas of raspberry, spice, and minerals. A hint of cherry pastry lingers in the finish. It tastes fruity and dry and has medium body that the small persistent bubbles lighten.
FOOD PAIRING: Deep-fried goat cheese with lavender honey. The wine holds its own against the cheese, and the fried batter augments the toasty notes of the wine.
PRICE: $12

Le Colture Rosé Vino Spumante Brut Veneto, Italy
Consisting of Chardonnay (70 percent) and Merlot
(30 percent), this wine is made with the Charmat Method
and has 9 grams of sugar per liter.

TASTING NOTES: Medium pink and fully sparkling, it smells of
strawberry and cherry with hints of flowers, almond, yellow
apple, and minerals. It tastes faintly sweet and has medium
body with balanced acidity made lighter by the bubbles.

FOOD PAIRING: Antipasti, such as hard provolone, roasted red
peppers, sun-dried tomatoes, and black olives. The foods'
saltiness and acidity nicely augment the fruit of the wine.

PRICE: $15

Piper-Heidsieck Rosé Sauvage Brut Champagne

Champagne, France

This sparkling wine consists mostly of Pinot Noir and Pinot Meunier and just 15 percent Chardonnay. Before the secondary fermentation in the bottle, the winemaker adds red wine to create the intense color and berry flavor. Then the wine ages on its lees for about two years.

TASTING NOTES: Bright rose pink with pronounced aromas of raspberry, cherry, blood orange, minerals, and a hint of spice. It tastes dry and has medium body lightened by the bubbles but plenty of fruit flavor with baked pastry notes in the finish.

FOOD PAIRING: Hors d'oeuvres, such as steak medallions topped with horseradish cream on toasted garlic crostini. The weight and fruit intensity of the wine dance well with the symphony of flavors in the food.

PRICE: $50

⑦

⇒ RICH ⇐

These wines have greater intensity and concentration of color, body, and flavor than the wines in the other categories because of the grapes used, growing regions, and winemaking style. If you fall into this category:

* You take your coffee black, no sugar, no milk, and the darker the better.
* It's dark chocolate or nothing.
* You prefer rich snacks, such as chocolate or fudge.
* You gravitate toward the more spicy or musky perfumes or colognes.
* You can handle your spirits—gin, tequila, vodka, whiskey—neat.

You may like wines that fall into other categories—particularly wines that have common characteristics. For example, you may enjoy the bold fruitiness of the Fruity style or the sweet intensity of the Blush category Remember, these categories offer rough palate guidelines to help you explore the vast, delicious world of wine.

RICH CHARACTERISTICS

* Deep pink color: These wines come from dark red grapes, are blended with rich red wine, or employ the saignée method. Deepness of color generally, though not always, indicates a wine's intensity of flavor.
* Dry: The level of residual sugar measures at fewer than 5 grams per liter. These wines sometimes can taste sweeter than they really are.
* Full body: Of all rosés, these wines have the fullest, richest mouthfeel.
* Warm alcohol: Generally 13.5% ABV or higher for this style. The higher the alcohol, the hotter it tastes. Also, note that on the palate alcohol can taste sweet while technically being dry.

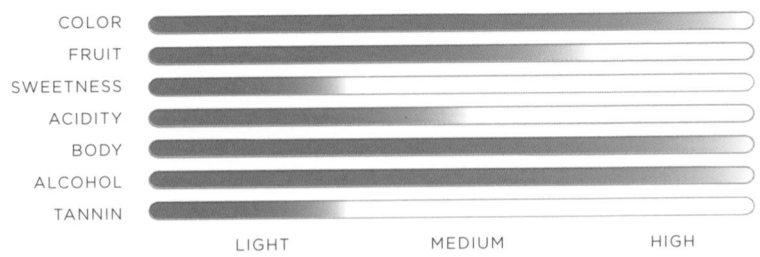

COLOR · FRUIT · SWEETNESS · ACIDITY · BODY · ALCOHOL · TANNIN

LIGHT · MEDIUM · HIGH

Warmer growing climates, thicker-skinned grapes, the saignée method, or length of maceration time characterize these wines. These techniques result in bold, dark, delicious, dense rosés that aren't for the timid!

TAVEL

This region lies within the southern Rhône Valley in France and embodies a quintessential wine style long overlooked until recently—probably because the area (just 3.6 square miles) produces very little wine, fewer than 500,000 cases per year. To put that into perspective: Barefoot Wines produced 17 million cases in 2015. This rosé has a much deeper color because winemakers here either combine red and white grapes together or blend light rosé must with darker rosé must before fermentation. The frequent inclusion of Grenache, which loves the sun and therefore has lots of sugar to convert into alcohol, gives this wine a high alcohol potential, between 11 and 13.5 percent by law. This higher alcohol level also gives the wine more body.

Le Chant du Soleil Tavel Rhône, France

This wine consists of decreasing amounts of Grenache, Cinsaut, Clairette, Syrah, and Piquepoul grapes.

TASTING NOTES: Deep rose color with intense aromas of raspberry and cherry and hints of blood orange, lavender, and rosemary. It's dry and full-bodied with warming alcohol and bitter cherry, spice, and a slight orange-peel bitterness in the finish—almost like a good cocktail.

FOOD PAIRING: Hamburger with Gruyère, caramelized onions, and garlic aioli. The wine makes the flavors of the food jump, and the protein of the burger softens some of the bitterness in the finish and makes the raspberry notes pop.

PRICE: $13

Château d'Aqueria Tavel Rhône, France

Growers harvest and destem the Grenache, Syrah, Cinsaut, Mourvèdre, Clairette, Bourboulenc, and Piquepoul grapes by hand, after which the grapes macerate for between twelve and thirty-six hours to extract color. The grapes then undergo pressing, temperature-controlled maceration, and fermentation in stainless-steel vats. The wine ages for six months on its lees in stainless steel.

TASTING NOTES: Deep fuchsia with intensely fragrant aromas of ripe wild strawberry, raspberry, lavender, and minerals. It has full body with a rich density, moderate acidity, and warming alcohol in the finish. Drink it in the fall or winter.

FOOD PAIRING: Salade Niçoise, which consists of medium-rare tuna, anchovies, hard-boiled eggs, Niçoise olives, and tomatoes all dressed with a vinaigrette.

PRICE: $20

BONUS TAVEL

Château de Segries Tavel Rhône, France

"This Tavel AOC has a distinct, deep, transparent, fruit punch–like color. The youthful nose carries notes of cherry, raspberry, lime, cranberry, and strawberry. The palate is dry with high acidity and alcohol and medium-full body. Wonderfully balanced, the pronounced flavors of cherry, cranberry, watermelon, strawberry, and rose delight."

PRICE: $18

—Thomas Erickson, Shanghai, China

FUN FACT

Legend has it that King Philip IV of France, who obliterated the Templars, traveled through Tavel on one of his royal tours. According to the story, he drank a glass of the local wine and proclaimed it the only good wine in the world. Tavel produces only rosé wines (which makes the phrase "Tavel rosé" redundant).

AGIORGITIKO ROZ

Greece has one of the oldest wine-producing traditions in the world, but it accounts for a drop in the bucket of world wine sales. Nevertheless, Greek wines and attention to them for their affordability and drinkability have surged in recent years. The most popular white variety consumed here is Moschofilero (a pink-hued grape, like Pinot Gris), and the leading red grape—in both plantings and consumption—is Agiorgitiko, which comes from the Peloponnese in southern Greece. Vintners use this grape to make a variety of styles, including highly prized, intensely dark and spicy reds and deeply colored, easy-to-drink rozes. These are some of the deepest rosés that you'll see. The warm Mediterranean climate and macerated dark grape make for an intense wine. Winemakers sometimes temper it with a little Moschofilero, which adds delicate floral notes to the otherwise bold finished product. Greek rozes offer great value for their price.

Domaine Skouras "Zoe" Rosé Peloponnese, Greece

The Agiorgitiko must (70 percent) undergoes skin contact for twenty-four to forty-eight hours at 64°F. For the Moschofilero (30 percent), skin contact for six hours at 43°F. The wine ferments in stainless-steel vats, has a short maceration, and ages briefly over fine lees.

TASTING NOTES: Bold reddish pink with aromas of fresh ripe juicy raspberry, cherry, and wild strawberry with hints of pear, rose petal, and minerals. This wine has medium-full body and rich, concentrated flavors with moderate acidity and alcohol.

FOOD PAIRING: Grilled chicken and zucchini on a roll with roasted red pepper mayonnaise. The chicken highlights the wine's fruit flavors, while the vegetables enhance the wine's floral and spice notes.

PRICE: $11

Tselepos Driopi Rosé Peloponnese, Greece

Agiorgitiko grapes undergo extraction for thirty-six hours before fermentation at a controlled temperature.

TASTING NOTES: Deep hot pink with intense aromas of fresh ripe raspberry, candied cherry, and a hint of spice and minerals. Dry and concentrated on the palate with balanced, refreshing acidity and moderate alcohol.

FOOD PAIRING: Baked Greek dishes, including spanakopita (filo dough filled with spinach and feta cheese and baked); savory meats, such as rosemary lamb or sweet fennel sausage; and hearty fish, such as tuna or salmon. Avoid white fish or light seafood, such as clams, oysters, and shrimp—all of which the wine will overpower.

PRICE: $13

FUN FACT

Agiorgitiko literally means "St. George's grape" and takes its name from a Greek soldier in the Roman army who was martyred in the reign of Emperor Diocletian.

SYRAH ROSÉ

This dark, thick-skinned variety makes some of the longest-lived wines from the Rhône Valley, such as Hermitage and Côte-Rôtie. It features notes of black pepper, and, when made into a rosé using maceration or saignée, it creates deep, rich rosés.

Francis Coppola Sofia Rosé Monterey County, California
The roughly even thirds of Syrah, Pinot Noir, and Grenache undergo crushing and destemming. For color extraction, the grapes cold-soak for forty-eight hours before the juice is separated from the skins. It cool-ferments to retain the fruit's aromatics.

TASTING NOTES: Deep rose pink with intense aromas of raspberry and wild strawberry, with hints of spice and floral notes in the finish. It has full body with juicy sweet fruit flavors and moderate alcohol (13% ABV).

FOOD PAIRING: Tacos or taco salad—chicken, romaine lettuce, grape tomatoes, corn, black beans, lime-chile dressing and (my secret ingredient) Doritos. This wine handles it all in stride.

PRICE: $15

Ampelos Rosé of Syrah Santa Barbara County, California
Syrah, Grenache, and Riesling ferment with native yeast
at 55°F in stainless-steel tanks.

TASTING NOTES: Bright fuchsia with dense aromas of
raspberry and spice. It tastes dry and has full body,
warming alcohol, and notes of raspberry, herbs, and
black spice. It also has an incredibly long finish.

FOOD PAIRING: Hamburger and fries or a fried chicken
sandwich. The wine's bright acid will cut through the fat
and have you begging for more.

PRICE: $23

MENCÍA ROSADO

Pink Spanish wines are nothing new, and if you've looked through the other style categories, you've already seen several: white grape Rioja rosado, red grape Spanish rosado, and txakolin gorria. Northern Spain made pale red, bright pink wines widely sought in the late Middle Ages. Various Spanish courts drank Cigales wines, probably the most historically famous of the bunch, from the thirteenth to the fifteenth centuries. Today Spain has begun capitalizing on its treasure trove of red grape varieties that can make deliciously bold, dry rosados. The Mencía grape grows in northwest Spain and in the Bierzo region makes deep, brooding, violet-scented red wines. When made into a saignée rosé, however, it boldly stands up to rich tapas and other delicious dishes.

Avancia Rosé of Mencía Valdeorras, Spain

Growers carefully harvest the grapes by hand from southerly hillsides. After a gentle crushing, the wine ferments in French oak barrels and ages on its lees for three months.

TASTING NOTES: Deep salmon pink with fragrant red berries on the nose. On the palate, it tastes dry with full body, warm alcohol, soft acidity, and a hint of blackberry compote and spice in the finish.

FOOD PAIRING: Beef or meat-based tapas, chili, or vegetarian chili. The spice in the wine's finish augments the cumin and smoky flavors in the chili, while its soft acidity won't strip the flavor. Just make sure the dish isn't too spicy, which will underscore the alcohol too much.

PRICE: $17

SAIGNÉE MERLOT AND MALBEC ROSÉ

Vintners can make Merlot into a variety of styles, depending on where it grows and what techniques they use. For rosé, we see white Merlot in the Blush style, direct press in the Crisp style, maceration in the Fruity style, and now the saignée method for the Rich style. Merlot and Malbec have some common characteristics with other thick-skinned varieties, such as Cabernet Sauvignon. They both fall firmly in the black fruit family when made into red wines, and they both have softer texture and acidity and a touch of violet in the bouquet—all of which presents even in Rich-style rosés made from them.

Maimai Rosé Hawke's Bay, New Zealand

Early in the fermentation, the color is bled off the juice and managed separately to retain the wine's freshness and fruitiness.

TASTING NOTES: Rich bright pink with aromas of cranberry, blood orange, black tea, and a hint of brown spice. It has round body, soft acidity, and warmly balanced alcohol. Imagine the end-of-year holidays in a bottle.

FOOD PAIRING: Rosemary lamb. The herb enhances the tea leaf and floral notes of the wine, while the protein highlights the wine's berry flavors.

PRICE: $16

Susana Balbo Crios Rosé of Malbec Mendoza, Argentina

Old-vine Malbec grapes go through the saignée method, and fermentation takes place in stainless-steel tanks.

TASTING NOTES: Bold pink with aromas of blackberry, plum, raspberry, and candied violet. On the palate, it's broad with soft acid and a warming finish. This is a perfect picnic wine whether outside or on your floor.

FOOD PAIRING: Pappardelle with sweet Italian sausage and peas in a tomato cream sauce. It's a big dish, make no mistake, but this rosé can handle it, and the sausage makes the dark plummy fruit of the wine stand out.

PRICE: $13

MOURVÈDRE ROSÉ

The Bandol region of Provence makes high-end red wine predominantly from Mourvèdre (Monastrell in Spain), another dark, thick-skinned grape known for its dark fruit aromas, such as blackberry and plum. Both the red and rosé wines made from this grape taste lush and rich—quite unlike the surrounding Provençal style. With short maceration or blended with Grenache, Mourvèdre tastes more fruity than rich. When long-macerated or made using the saignée method, however, it falls firmly in the Rich style.

Fausse Piste Rosé of Mourvèdre

Rogue Valley, Oregon

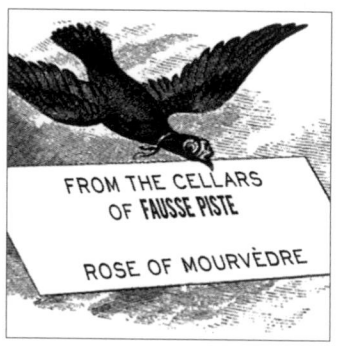

After three days of maceration, the Mourvèdre must undergoes pressing and then ferments in old wooden barrels from the Rhône Valley. TASTING NOTES: Orange-pink in color with an intensely plummy nose and notes of tea leaf and spice. Lush and full-bodied, it has a soft texture, low acidity, and modest alcohol (10.5% ABV).

FOOD PAIRING: Braised beef short ribs—no barbecue sauce, though. The richness of the ribs augments the wine's fruit flavor, and the wine enhances the rich meaty flavor of the dish.

PRICE: $18

Château de Pibarnon Bandol Rosé Provence, France

Pibarnon sits at Bandol's highest point, roughly 1,000 feet above sea level. The Mediterranean and altitude moderate temperatures, and the estate's rare and mineral-rich soils, called Trias, retain water even in the driest years. This wine interestingly blends the direct press and saignée methods. Cinsaut grapes (35 percent) undergo pressing, while Mourvèdre grapes (65 percent) go into a tank, from which the winemaker draws the free-run juice. After fermentation with indigenous yeasts in stainless-steel tanks, the wines are blended and age for six months in tanks.

TASTING NOTES: Salmon pink with notes of tulip, rose, cranberry, and plum with hints of minerals. It tastes dry and has medium-light body with dense flavors and soft acidity.

FOOD PAIRING: Sushi, particularly a tuna or California roll, or Chicken Teriyaki.

PRICE: $28

SAIGNÉE GSM ROSÉ

If the grapes of a GSM blend undergo direct pressing, the wine can and often does fall into the Crisp category. If they see short maceration, it goes in Fruity. When long-macerated or bled from the red wine tank, it lands firmly in the Rich style. Grenache, the lead grape in the blend, imparts more red berry flavors, such as cherry, than other wines in this chapter.

Crux GSM Rosé Russian River Valley, Sonoma County, California
This wine contains half Grenache, a third Syrah, and the rest Mourvèdre.
TASTING NOTES: Deep coral color with intense aromas of cherry, watermelon, and hints of black pepper. It has full body with a soft texture and a spicy warming finish.
FOOD PAIRING: Caesar salad with or without grilled chicken.
PRICE: $24

LONG MACERATION

Where does rosé end and red wine begin? The lines—more artistic expression than concrete demarcation—blur. Some winemakers in the New World use thin-skinned grapes, such as Pinot Noir, to make wine that you might categorize as a rosé or a red. Best to check the label.

Antica Terra Angelicall Rosé

Eola-Amity Hills, Oregon

This wine takes its name from the Angelicall Stone, a mythic substance sought by alchemists. The Pinot Noir grapes macerate on their skins for a little more than a week. After fermentation, the wine ages in barrels on its lees for a year before bottling.

TASTING NOTES: Deep rose pink or pale ruby color with intense aromas of wild strawberry, cherry, and forest floor, with a hint of orange blossom and vanilla spice. It's full-bodied for a rosé with moderate acidity and a long, warming finish.

FOOD PAIRING: Duck, one of the best pairings for red Burgundy (also Pinot Noir).

PRICE: $90

NEW WORLD CABERNET SAUVIGNON ROSÉ

This thick-skinned grape makes some of the richest, most powerful, most famous, longest-lived, most expensive red wines in the world. On its own, it has a strong taste of black currant or cassis. Sometimes that taste leans toward green bell pepper, while at other times it tastes faintly herbal. Rosés made from Cabernet Sauvignon tend to appear darker and always feature this herbaceousness.

Viña La Playa Cabernet Sauvignon Rosé Colchagua Valley, Chile
Blended with 15 percent Viognier, this wine ferments at 54–57°F for twelve days in stainless-steel tanks.

TASTING NOTES: Pink salmon color with fragrant aromas of red currant, black currant, white flowers, and a hint of green bell pepper. It's quite dry with medium weight, roundness (likely from the Viognier), and vibrant acidity. It finishes with clean raspberry and cherry fruit and a touch of spice at the very end.

FOOD PAIRING: Beef empanadas (a savory fried stuffed pastry).
PRICE: $9

Isabel Mondavi Deep Rosé Napa Valley, California

Named for Isabel Mondavi, wife of Michael and mother of Robert and Dina, this wine originally was envisioned as "just a few cases for Mom," but it grew. Isabel's love of food-and-wine pairings for entertaining led to this style of flavorful wines created in her name. TASTING NOTES: This is one of the deepest rosés you'll ever see, and it looks darker than many Pinot Noirs. It has rich, concentrated aromas of black currant and raspberry jam with notes of brown spice. It also has the fullest body of any rosé in this book with moderately low acidity and a long, warming finish.

FOOD PAIRING: Steak fajitas, grilled chicken, or prime rib—nothing with delicate flavors.

PRICE: $16

SAIGNÉE ROSÉ CHAMPAGNE

Most sparkling wines go through two fermentations. With the saignée method, the red grapes don't undergo direct pressing but macerate and ferment with the skins, which allows the color to bleed into the wine. This step happens before the secondary fermentation, resulting in a richer, bolder, more robust, deeply flavored sparkling rosé in contrast to the crisp delicateness of blanc de noirs or the curvier softness of a traditional sparkling rosé.

Gratiot Désiré Rosé de Saignée Extra Brut

Champagne, France

Extra brut can taste brutally tart, but the rich fruit concentration and color place this wine firmly in the Rich category. Made of 60 percent Pinot Noir, 30 percent Pinot Meunier, and 10 percent Chardonnay, the wine rests for four years on its lees.

TASTING NOTES: Deep fuchsia with strong aromas of cranberry, raspberry, freesia, baked bread, and chalky minerality. It tastes very dry and very crisp with tiny, persistent bubbles and a long, lingering finish.

FOOD PAIRING: Fried scallops or duck. The wine's high acidity tempers the rich fattiness of the duck or the slight sweetness of the scallops, preparing you for another bite.

PRICE: $42

RESOURCES

8

FOOD PAIRING GUIDE

My wine epiphany took place during a business lunch in London, where people take a more relaxed view of casual drinking during the workday. The restaurant served an herb-crusted salmon with a Sancerre, a Sauvignon Blanc from the Loire Valley in France. On its own, the wine didn't impress me, but the combination of the fish and wine blew me away. In that moment, it occurred to me that the chef didn't think *Oh, it doesn't matter, just give them the Sancerre*. Someone made a conscious decision to put them together.

That moment convinced me that I had to take a wine class. One class led to another and began my career in wine, which I now taste for a living (best job ever!). That food-and-wine pairing changed my life.

TYPES OF PAIRINGS

About five years ago, I cowrote *Pairing with the Masters* with Certified Master Chef Ken Arnone. Given the intricacy of the recipes and the rigorous, exhaustive—albeit delicious—testing, that book took three years to write. With the wisdom of that experience, we organized pairings into three distinct types.

One-Way Pairing

In this pairing, either the food makes the wine taste better, or the wine makes the food taste better—but not both. Pairing rosé champagne with lobster in butter sauce offers a good example. The champagne's tangy minerality and crisp acidity make the lobster's flavor shine, but the lobster doesn't really do anything for the wine. In this case, the wine made the food taste better. The pairing goes only one way.

Two-Way Pairing

In this pairing, unsurprisingly, the food makes the wine taste better, and the wine makes the food taste better. Consider a meat ravioli en brodo paired with a Costières de Nîmes rosé, similar to a crisp Provence rosé. The wine's berry flavors contrast beautifully with the rich savory flavor of the meat, which in turn tastes more flavorful alongside the rosé. Meanwhile, the herbs used to flavor the meat and the broth accent the herbal elements in the wine, making the wine taste more complex than it does on its own.

Another great example: Tavel paired with a chicken salad with apples, cranberries, and pecans. The cranberries create a taste bridge that complements the rich red berry notes of the wine; the wine's crisp acidity and berry flavors contrast with the flavors of the chicken; and the richness of the mayonnaise elongates everything on the palate for a satisfying finish.

Three-Way Pairing

It may sound like the start of a blue joke, but in some pairings the food makes the wine taste better, the wine makes the food taste better, and the combination creates something new and almost magical. Think about chocolate and peanut butter. Each tastes great on its own, but together they create something richer and more delicious than either one individually. For a more decadent example, try bourbon with salted caramel ice cream.

The pairing of Amarone, a rich red wine from Italy, and pasta carbonara has all the flavors that the palate can perceive: sweet, sour, salty, bitter, and umami. The dish focuses the wine, which contrasts with the food, and everything pops. Also try Ruby Port with milk or dark chocolate. It's a match made in heaven. Don't believe me? Try it, and then try a dry champagne with chocolate.

FAT FACT

Fat elongates flavor. Because fat doesn't dissolve as quickly as sugar or other ingredients, the flavor lingers on your palate. This probably explains why everything tastes better with butter, mayonnaise, olive oil, or other kinds of fat.

WHAT MAKES GREAT PAIRINGS

Originally I organized this section by weight, texture, and flavor but quickly realized that the abbreviation would be WTF—not the best mnemonic! Try BCC instead.

Balance

Let's start with the easiest part, balancing the weight of a dish with the weight of a wine. Remember the analogy from the tasting chapter: body in wine is like body in milk: skim, whole, and heavy cream. The texture and flavors differ of course, but the feeling of the weight on your palate follows the same principle, and the same applies to dishes. A balanced food-and-wine pairing matches wine and food of equal body or weight, so you balance a light dish with a light wine and so on. A full-bodied wine, such as a rich Cabernet Sauvignon, would overpower a light fish, such as tilapia, flounder, or sea bass. Think of it like a dance between one tall and large person and a small, petite person. Chances are the big dancer will step on the toes of and overwhelm the small dancer. That's what happens when you mismatch food and wine by body.

The good news for rosé is that it has a more narrow and predictable range than other categories of wine. Rosés in the Crisp style resemble a light white wine in body, while even the fullest-bodied rosés in the Rich style are akin to the light end of the spectrum of red wine. This happily makes it easier to pair rosé with a wider range of foods than either white or red wine alone.

Complement

Flavor complementing is when a food flavor parallels a wine flavor, creating a bridge between them. Rosé made from Syrah, for example, can have some black spice aromas. Pair it with a dish that has some light black pepper flavor, such as lamb au poivre, and the two tastes enhance each other.

Be careful, though, that you don't compound flavors by accident. Compounding is when a flavor overcomplements itself in a pairing, and that's all you can taste. A good example is a Loire Cabernet Franc from a cool vintage, which creates "green" flavors in the wine, paired with a chicken breast stuffed with spinach. The herbal flavors of the wine when combined with the spinach make the pairing taste overwhelmingly vegetal, obscuring the other flavors.

Contrast

Flavor contrasting is when two flavors differ in such a way that enhances both. When you pair a Fruity-style rosé with a savory dish, such as poached salmon, the meaty taste of the salmon contrasts with the berry fruit in the rosé, which makes both sets of flavors pop.

Be careful here, as well, that you don't go too far and veer into clashing, which is when flavors differ so much that they fight each other. The weights of a Pink Moscato and a pork tenderloin with caramelized apple compote might match each other, but the sweet, acidic compote will make the perfumey, floral flavors of the wine taste like soap.

BAD PAIRINGS

Sometimes it helps to know what constitutes a bad pairing in order to help make good ones. Have you ever tasted orange juice immediately after brushing your teeth? That bitter, sour sensation offers a good example of clashing flavors that make your palate wince. Some food-and-wine pairings naturally create chemical reactions that taste awful. For example, sea bass with Pinot Noir creates a metallic taste. This isn't to say that, if it's not awful, it's a good pairing. In neutral pairings, there's no harm done, but nothing improves either.

CHOOSE THE RIGHT WINE

Most of the time we decide what to eat first and select the wine to go along with it. If you know what you're going to eat, keep these points in mind when choosing a rosé:

* AVOID WINES TOO SWEET FOR THE DISH. Some Blush-style wines may taste too sweet for some dishes. For example, you may think that a sweet cranberry-style wine will complement a chicken salad with cranberries and pecans, but its intense sweetness can overpower and cover the flavor of the dish, making everything taste candied.
* AVOID WINES TOO RICH FOR THE DISH. Some Rich-style wines may taste too intense for a mild or delicate dish. The heavy weight of the wine can overwhelm the subtle flavors of the food. Choose a delicate Crisp-style wine with a light-bodied dish.
* CONSIDER ACIDITY. Rosés in the Crisp style often are fairly delicate and have high acidity. Two problems can arise if acidity levels don't align properly.
  * *Stripping.* Putting lemon on your fish, chicken, or green beans highlights the more delicate flavors in the food. Too much, however, will strip the flavor from your palate. For example, a pale blanc de noirs champagne with salmon may create a pleasing cleansing sensation initially, but the salmon flavor soon disappears.
  * *Compounding.* Imagine having ceviche—raw seafood cured by citrus juices—with a crisp Pinot Noir rosé. The weights match, but the high acidity of the wine plus the acid in the dish makes everything taste sour. Better to pair ceviche with a Blush or Fruity style rosé with softer acidity.

MAKE A DISH MORE WINE FRIENDLY

If, in the other direction, you want to match your food to a wine that you want to drink or that you've received as a gift, it's much easier to change the dish. Here are some steps you can take to make a dish more wine friendly:

* AVOID SWEETNESS FOR DRY ROSÉS. Dry rosés (in the Crisp, Fruity, and Rich styles) can taste sour when paired with dishes that have a strong element of sweetness, such as a sweet sauce. Even a Blush-style wine can seem sour if the dish tastes sweeter than the wine.
* AVOID HOT SPICES FOR DRY ROSÉS. Spices that create a heat sensation can enhance the taste of alcohol and bitterness in a wine, particularly for Fruity- and Rich-style rosés. Spices also can obscure flavors for Crisp-style rosés. Blush-style rosés work quite well with spices, though. The sweetness calms the heat, and the spice can enhance the fruit component of the wine—so go crazy!
* AVOID BITTER INGREDIENTS. A good chef considers the balance among acid, bitterness, flavor, weight, etc. Some elements that can balance a dish may create astringency when paired with a wine, however. Consider broccoli rabe, a semi-bitter vegetable. If you have a dish with broccoli rabe in it and pair it with a Rich-style rosé, the combination will create a harsh bitterness on your palate.

DON'T WORRY

The point of wine is to enjoy drinking it, so in the end only what you like matters. Don't let anyone tell you differently.

A few years ago, Chef Arnone and I did a food-and-wine pairing dinner called "The Good, the Bad, and the Ugly." The point was to pair one dish with different wines to demonstrate good pairings and a truly awful one. For the awful pairing, we paired kung pao shrimp with a Barolo, a rich red wine from Italy with high acidity, high alcohol, and high tannins. We figured that the intense heat from the spicy food would make the wine taste acrid and harsh, like rocket fuel. At the end of the night, though, when the room voted on best and worst pairings, five people cited that combination as their absolute favorite!

Were they wrong? Of course not; the question was a matter of taste. Each of the five explained that he or she didn't care about the dish. It didn't matter what they ate; they could have eaten cardboard, and the pairing still would have been their favorite because they adored Barolo!

The lesson? Pairing guidelines are just that—guidelines rather than rules.

PRONUNCIATION GUIDE

ABRUZZO: ah-BROOT-zo

AGIORGITIKO: ah-yor-YEE-tee-ko

ALENTEJO: ahl-en-TAY-zhoo

AMARONE: ah-mah-ROH-nay

AU POIVRE: oh PWAHV-ruh

BANDOL: bahn-DOL

BEAUJOLAIS: bo-zhuh-LAY

BLANC DE NOIRS:
blahnk duh NWAHR

BOCKSBEUTEL: BOHKS-boy-tuhl

BRACHETTO: brah-KEHT-toh

CABERNET FRANC:
kab-uhr-NAY FRAHNK

CABERNET SAUVIGNON:
kab-uhr-NAY so-vin-YOHN

CARIÑENA: kahr-in-YAY-nah

CATALONIA: kat-uh-LOHN-yuh

CAVA: KAH-vuh

CERASUOLO: chehr-ah-SWO-lo

CHARMAT: shahr-MAH

CHIARETTO: kee-ah-REHT-toh

CHINON: shee-NOHN

CINSAUT: SAN-so

CLARET: KLA-ret

CLARETE: klah-RAY-tay

COLCHAGUA: cohl-CHAH-gwah

COONAWARA: coon-ah-WEHR-uh

COQUILLE D'OC: ko-KEE dok

COSTIÈRES DE NÎMES:
    kost-ee-YEHR duh NEEM

CÔTE D'AZUR: koht dah-ZOOR

COTEAUX D'AIX EN PROVENCE:
    koh-toh DEX ahn pro-VONS

CÔTES DE TOUL: koht duh TOOL

CRAYÈRES: cray-YEHR

DOSAGE: doh-SAZH

FINO: FEE-no

FRIZZANTE: free-ZAHN-tay

GAMAY: GA-may

GARNACHA: gar-NAH-cha

GEWÜRZTRAMINER:
    geh-VURTS-trah-MEEN-uhr

GRENACHE: gruh-NAHSH

GRÜNER VELTLINER:
    GROO-nuhr VELT-leen-uhr

HANDARRIBI BELTZA:
    hahn-dahr-REE-bee BEHLT-zuh

HONDARRABI ZURI:
    hahn-dahr-REE-bee SOO-ree

JUMILLA: hoo-MEE-yuh

LORRAINE: lo-REHN

MALBEC: MAHL-bek

MATARO: mah-tah-RO

MATEUS: mah-TOOS

MENCÍA: mehn-THEE-uh

MERLOT: muhr-LO

MONASTRELL: mohn-ah-STRELL

MONTEPULCIANO:
    MOHN-tay-pool-CHAH-no

MOSCATO: mo-SKAH-to

MOSCHOFILERO:
    MOSS-ko-fee-LEHR-oh

MOURVÈDRE: moor-VEHD-ruh

MURCIA: MOOR-see-uh

MUSCADET: moos-kah-DAY

MUSCAT: MUH-skaht

NEGROAMARO: NEHG-ro-ah-MAH-ro

NERELLO MASCALESE:
    neh-REHL-lo mask-ah-LAY-say

PAUILLAC: poy-YAK

PINOT GRIGIO: PEE-no GREE-jo

PINOT GRIS: PEE-no GREE

PINOT NOIR: PEE-no NWAHR

PROVENÇAL: pro-von-SAHL

PROVENCE: pro-VONS

RHEINGAU: RINE-gow

RHÔNE: ROHN

RIOJA: ree-OH-hah

ROSADO: ro-SAH-doh

ROSATO: ro-SAH-toh

ROSÉ: ro-ZAY

SAIGNÉE: sehn-YAY

SANCERRE: sahn-SEHR

SANGIOVESE: SAHN-jo-VAY-say

SANGRÍA: sahn-GREE-ah

SHIRAZ: sheer-AHZ, sheer-AZ

SOMMELIER: so-mehl-YAY

SPUMANTE: spoo-MAHN-tay

ST. TROPEZ: sahn tro-PAY

SYRAH: suhr-AH

TAVEL: tah-VEHL

TEMPRANILLO: TEHM-prah-NEE-yo

TIBOUREN: tee-boo-REHN

TOURIGA NACIONAL:
too-REE-gah NAHS-yo-NAHL

TOURRAINE: too-REHN

TXAKOLINA: chah-ko-LEE-nah

UMAMI: oo-MAH-mee

VALDEORRAS: vahl-day-OR-rahs

VALDIGUIÉ: vahl-dee-ghee-AY

VALPOLICELLA:
VAHL-po-lee-CHEHL-ah

VENETO: VEHN-eh-toh

VIELLES VIGNES: vyay VEEN

VIN GRIS: van GREE

VINHO VERDE: VEEN-yo vehr-DAY

VITIS VINIFERA: VIT-is vin-IF-ehr-ah

ZINFANDEL: ZIN-fahn-dehl

ZWEIGELT: TSVY-guhlt

WINE CHECKLIST

Blush

- ❑ André Strawberry Moscato Sparkling
- ❑ Barefoot Bubbly Pink Moscato Sparkling Champagne
- ❑ Broadbent Vinho Verde Rosé
- ❑ California Wine Co. Cranberry Wine
- ❑ Cantine Riondo Pink Spago Argento
- ❑ Elio Perrone Bigaro Frizzante
- ❑ Gallo Family White Merlot
- ❑ Gekkeikan Plum Wine
- ❑ Hello Kitty Sparkling Rosé
- ❑ LVP Pink Sangria
- ❑ Pindar Summer Blush
- ❑ Rosa Regale Banfi Brachetto d'Aqui Spumante
- ❑ Roscato Rosé Dolce
- ❑ Sogrape Mateus "The Original"
- ❑ Sutter Home White Zinfandel

Crisp

- ☐ Ameztoi Getariako Txakolina Rubentis
- ☐ Carmel Road Barrymore Rosé of Pinot Noir
- ☐ Clos Cibonne Tibouren Tradition Rosé
- ☐ Conundrum Rosé
- ☐ Costaripa RosaMara Valtènesi Chiaretto Garda Classico
- ☐ CVNE Viña Real Rosado
- ☐ Domaine Fontaine du Clos Rosé
- ☐ Domaine La Rabiotte Rosé de Provence
- ☐ Domaines Ott Mireille Clair de Noirs
- ☐ Egly-Ouriet Blanc de Noirs Grand Cru Les Crayères Vielles Vignes
- ☐ Herdade do Rocim "Mariana" Rosé
- ☐ J. Mourat Collection Rosé
- ☐ Lelièvre de Vin Gris de Toul
- ☐ Michel Chapoutier Tournon Mathilda Rosé
- ☐ Pascal et Nicolas Reverdy Sancerre Terre de Maimbray Rosé
- ☐ Petra Unger "Q" Rosé
- ☐ Raidis Estate Pinot Gris Rosé Cheeky Goat
- ☐ René Jolly Blanc de Noirs Brut Champagne
- ☐ Saint Aix AIX Rosé
- ☐ Schramsberg Blanc de Noirs Brut Vintage
- ☐ Smith Story Rosé of Pinot Noir
- ☐ Wölffer Estate Rosé

Fruity

- ☐ Badenhorst Family Wines Secateurs Rosé
- ☐ Bodegas Olivares Jumilla Rosado
- ☐ Cantele Negroamaro Rosato
- ☐ Château de Sours La Fleur d'Amelie Bordeaux Rosé
- ☐ Le Colture Rosé Vino Spumante Brut
- ☐ El Coto Rioja Rosado
- ☐ Domaine Clarence Dillon Clarendelle Rosé
- ☐ Domaine de Sainte Rose Coquille d'Oc
- ☐ Domaine du Grand Breviande Chinon Rosé
- ☐ Fantini Farnese Cerasuolo d'Abruzzo
- ☐ Flam Rosé
- ☐ Girolamo Russo Etna Rosato
- ☐ La Granja 360 Garnacha Rosé
- ☐ Pata Negra Cava Rosé Brut
- ☐ Piper-Heidsieck Rosé Sauvage Brut Champagne
- ☐ Le P'tit Paysan Pierre's Pirouette Rosé of Mourvèdre
- ☐ Il Poggione Brancato Rosato di Toscana

Rich

- ☐ Ampelos Rosé of Syrah
- ☐ Antica Terra Angelicall Rosé
- ☐ Avancia Rosé of Mencía
- ☐ Le Chant du Soleil Tavel
- ☐ Château d'Aqueria Tavel
- ☐ Château de Pibarnon Bandol Rosé
- ☐ Château de Segries Tavel
- ☐ Crux GSM Rosé
- ☐ Domaine Skouras "Zoe" Rosé
- ☐ Fausse Piste Rosé of Mourvèdre,
- ☐ Francis Coppola Sofia Rosé
- ☐ Gratiot Désiré Rosé de Saignée Extra Brut
- ☐ Isabel Mondavi Deep Rosé
- ☐ Maimai Rosé
- ☐ Susana Balbo Crios Rosé of Malbec
- ☐ Tselepos Driopi Rosé
- ☐ Viña La Playa Cabernet Sauvignon Rosé

ACKNOWLEDGMENTS

Many have provided inspiration and motivation in the creation of this book.

I thank my darling husband, Christopher, for his unconditional love, devotion, friendship, and support. Everyone should be as blessed as I am to have such an incredibly supportive and loving spouse. This book would not have been possible without his passion for the idea and me.

I thank my family for their love, support, and enthusiasm. My mother, Michele, has a gift. If she can taste a dish, she can make it with no recipe, and her love of food and taste sensations started me on my path in the first place. I thank my father for instilling in me an unwavering discipline and focus. I aspire to his level of integrity and honor in all things. Additionally, I thank my sisters, Elizabeth and Katherine, for their creativity, inspiration, and ability always to lift my spirits.

I thank my grandparents. My grandfather Joseph began a successful writing career in his seventies and inspired me to write this book. My grandmother Caroline taught me never to give up. I also thank my grandfather Felix, who always said that I "can do," and my grandmother Arlene for reminding me always to have a little fun.

I thank Kevin Zraly. His energy and passion for wine ignited me, like so many of his students of the Windows on the World Wine School. His encouragement, kindness, and support have helped me get to where I am today.

Finally, to the countless friends, peers, and colleagues who have influenced and supported me, I thank you.

IMAGE CREDITS

We would like to thank all of the wineries and individuals who provided images for use in this book. All images copyright of the corresponding wineries with the following additions:

Cover: © Raffaele Montillo/Image Brief (front); © Heather Hussey Van Gaale/Image Brief (back)

Phil Adams: 115; Alamy: © Trinity Mirror/Mirrorpix: 8; Courtesy the Author: 176; Juan Canicio: 119; Inaki Caperochipi: 106; Claire Dattas: 91; Depositphotos: © Natalia Lisovskaya: 43 top; Domaine Skouras: Costas Mitropoulos: 138, 152–153; E. & J. Gallo Winery: Jesse Alvarez: 82; Fantini Farnese: viii; Getty Images: © Jan Caudron: 34;

© Philip Ramey: 10, © RDA/Hulton Archive: 7; Image Brief: © Ramón López Farinós: 43 bottom, © Tigran Hayrapetya: 52, © Iuliia Malivanchuk: 45 bottom, © Daniel Séguin: ii–iii, © Heather Hussey Van Gaale: vi; iStockphoto: © Eric Ferguson: v, © gilaxia: 13, 44, 45 top, © oersin: 64–65; Le Colture: 16; Geoff Nilsen: 150 top; Courtesy Pacific Prime Wines: Tony Speakman Photo & Design: 143; Gary Piazza: 147; Piper-Heidsieck: 29; Amy Ripplinger: 84; Shutterstock: © Natalia Lisovskaya: 162; StockFood: © Hans-Peter Siffert: 55; Stocksy; © Helen Rushbrook: 154; © Jeff Wasserman: 32; Jason Tinacci: 95; Tselepos Winery: 20; Sogrape Vinhos: Sérgio Ferreira: 72; Stacy Wickham Photography: 81; Courtesy Wikimedia Foundation: Mossot: 5; Wölffer Estate: 14–15, 26

INDEX

ABOUT THE AUTHOR

Jennifer Simonetti-Bryan is a master of wine, the world's top wine credential, and only the fourth woman in America to achieve that qualification. Author of *The One Minute Wine Master* (Sterling Epicure), she judges wine and spirits competitions worldwide, holds five additional wine and spirits certifications, and won the 2008 Tasting Trophy from the Institute of Masters of Wine. She has trained thousands of professionals in the hospitality industry and hosted seminars with Rachael Ray, Bobby Flay, Mario Batali, and other Food Network stars. She has appeared on TV (*Anderson Cooper*, Bloomberg TV, *Fox & Friends*, *Fox Business*, *Fox News*, *Today*); on the radio (Bloomberg, Martha Stewart, Sirius XM); and in print (*BusinessWeek*, *Food & Wine*, *Fortune*, *Gotham*, *Oprah*, *Reuters*, *Wall Street Journal*, *Wine Enthusiast*, *Wine Spectator*, and *Women's Health*). She lives with her husband in Los Angeles, California.